Cambridge Elements

Elements in Applied Linguistics
edited by
Li Wei
University College London
Zhu Hua
University College London

MULTIMODALITY AND TRANSLANGUAGING IN VIDEO INTERACTIONS

Maria Grazia Sindoni
University of Messina

Shaftesbury Road, Cambridge CB2 8EA, United Kingdom

One Liberty Plaza, 20th Floor, New York, NY 10006, USA

477 Williamstown Road, Port Melbourne, VIC 3207, Australia

314–321, 3rd Floor, Plot 3, Splendor Forum, Jasola District Centre,
New Delhi – 110025, India

103 Penang Road, #05–06/07, Visioncrest Commercial, Singapore 238467

Cambridge University Press is part of Cambridge University Press & Assessment,
a department of the University of Cambridge.

We share the University's mission to contribute to society through the pursuit of
education, learning and research at the highest international levels of excellence.

www.cambridge.org
Information on this title: www.cambridge.org/9781009454162

DOI: 10.1017/9781009286947

First published 2023

A catalogue record for this publication is available from the British Library

ISBN 978-1-009-45416-2 Hardback
ISBN 978-1-009-28692-3 Paperback
ISSN 2633-5069 (online)
ISSN 2633-5050 (print)

Additional resources for this publication at www.cambridge.org/Sindoni

Multimodality and Translanguaging in Video Interactions

Elements in Applied Linguistics

DOI: 10.1017/9781009286947
First published online: November 2023

Maria Grazia Sindoni
University of Messina

Author for correspondence: Maria Grazia Sindoni, mgsindoni@unime.it

Abstract: This Element presents and critically discusses video-mediated communication by combining theories and empirical methods of multimodal studies and translanguaging. Since the Covid-19 pandemic gained momentum, video-based interactions have become more and more ingrained in private and public lives, to the point of being fully incorporated in a wide range of community practices in personal, work, and educational environments. The meaning making of video communication results from the complex, situationally based, and culturally influenced and interlaced components of different semiotic resources and practices. These include the use of speech, writing, translingual practices, gaze behaviour, proxemics and kinesics patterns, as well as forms of embodied interaction. The Element aims at unpacking these resources and at interpreting how they make meanings, in order to improve and encourage active and responsible participation in the current digital scenarios.

Keywords: multimodality, translanguaging, video-mediated interactions, video communication, digital literacies

ISBNs: 9781009454162 (HB), 9781009286923 (PB), 9781009286947 (OC)
ISSNs: 2633-5069 (online), 2633-5050 (print)

Contents

1 Introduction

From the city where I live, Messina, located in the strait bearing the same name, which separates the Tyrrheanian Sea from the Ionian Sea in the Mediterranean, it is practically impossible to find oneself beyond the reach of the sea. It is everywhere – there is no way to escape sea views. During the first long lockdown we experienced in Italy back in 2020, I joined an online video meeting from my terrace to breathe some fresh air; a colleague of mine captured a glimpse of the holiday-like scenario of the mesmerizing sea of the Messina Strait and commented with a smirk: 'I see you're treating yourself well!' I stood in embarrassed silence, with a mounting sense of 'academic guilt' rapidly taking possession of me. This comment quite neatly captures a range of the sociological, sociosemiotic and interactional transformations that the Covid-19 pandemic has brought to the fore, most notably connected to the unprecedented ubiquity of live video calls. Video-mediated communication (VMC) has become so ingrained in the lives of so many people in an abrupt way that various social norms have been turned upside down, such as the normalized possibility to peep into other people's personal spaces, catching – and interpreting – private details, moments of awkward silences or unwanted intrusions from family members, pets, noisy neighbours and so on. Technologies have rapidly responded by further implementing already existing conversational affordances (Hutchby, 2001), such as the blurring background functionality or a webcam that detects unwanted intruders. However, the public invasion of the private has been legitimized to such an extent that reflection on what video communication now means is a requirement in various contexts (professional, educational, personal and so on) and in relation to various configurations (one-to-one, one-to-many, open-ended, etc.).

The Covid-19 pandemic, however, has accelerated a process well underway before the current explosion of the video-conferencing market. The global value of the video market was estimated at $4.21 billion in 2020, but is expected to have more than doubled by 2028, almost topping $10 billion, considering projections only for the United States, Canada, the United Kingdom, Germany, China, India, Japan and Brazil (Gran View Research, 2022). According to Statista (2022), Zoom topped the records with 129 million downloads of the app in 2020 for the Asia–Pacific, 113 million for the Americas, and almost 89 million for Europe, the Middle East and Africa combined. The peak reached in video communication in 2020 is of no interest in itself, as an increase in any particular form of interaction – mediated or otherwise – does not necessarily entail a change in discourse practices, media ideologies or interactional dynamics (Sindoni & Moschini, 2021a). Yet some contingencies attract attention and call for further investigation, such as the abrupt transition from offline to online of a multitude of activities, ranging from the personal, such as keeping in touch with loved ones, to the professional, such as participating in work meetings or developing tasks remotely. In addition, as mentioned already, video calls have blurred the previous clear-cut line (at least for most workers in both affluent and non-affluent countries) between personal and public spaces.

Educational contexts have been particularly affected by these changes. All the individuals involved in this sudden change of scenario, with no ready-made plan on how to transfer offline to online at all levels of education, including teachers, students and parents, have expressed concerns about the lack of a fully sustained support model from public and private educational institutions. The research literature is rapidly growing and overall describes the effects on education, frequently defining the learning and teaching experience mediated by video systems of teleconferencing as problematic, even though some aspects linked to remote instruction have been shown to enhance all participants' experiences (Rapanta et al., 2020). The challenges appear to be pretty similar at a global level, albeit with differently nuanced technological versus other logistical issues. Common problems include lack of sufficient institutional and financial support to buy equipment (especially infrastructure in non-affluent countries), as well as deficiencies in practical training (Joshi, Vinay & Bhaskar, 2021) and in guidance on how to 'redesign' learning under the new circumstances (Lim, 2021). Several studies have reported on specific contextual aspects, such as teachers' challenges in India (Joshi, Vinay & Bhaskar, 2021), in Western Canada (Code, Ralph & Forde, 2020) and in Latin American countries (i.e., Argentina, Ecuador, Chile and Peru, in Mateus et al., 2022), as well as students' perceptions in universities in Romania (Coman et al., 2020) and China (Li, 2022). A spotlight has been placed on how diverse forms of video communication have impacted on learning, for example within the employment of live, pre-recorded or hybrid video learning in China (Wang et al., 2022) or on how live-conferencing video systems can be used to support pre-service teachers in Australia (Maher, 2022).

Private and public educational institutions have embraced, subsumed and ultimately normalized new practices on a global scale. However, even though this unexpected transition has been partly discussed with regard to technical and pedagogical issues, little debate has been devoted to how video-mediated teaching and learning *semiotically differs* from offline traditional learning scenarios. An explanation for this state of affairs may be that synchronous VMC *seems to replicate* class dynamics at a distance, but, on closer inspection, one perceives that the distinct ways in which semiotic resources are deployed do in fact greatly influence how messages are exchanged and understood by both teachers and learners.

1.1 A Brief Overview of Research on VMC

The literature on VMC in the social sciences with a focus on language and meaning making is practically endless and cannot be summarized in a few pages, owing to the vast range of disciplines (e.g., applied linguistics, pragmatics, experimental psychology, interactional sociolinguistics, linguistic anthropology, media studies, digital ethnography), theories and empirical methodologies (e.g., conversation analysis, mediated discourse theory, multimodal discourse analysis, translanguaging, etc.) and scenarios (e.g., educational, professional, clinical, legal, personal) involved. This section will thus only mention a limited number of studies that, far from fully mapping the extremely wide area of VMC as a meaning-making event *and* as a practice, will help readers pinpoint areas of special interest for this domain, as it has been evolving in the last two decades.

From a theoretical standpoint, several disciplines and approaches have tackled VMC since its emergence in the electronic arena of the Internet. Early research on VMC was focused on comparisons between face-to-face communication and VMC in synchronous or asynchronous contexts, for example in experimental psychology settings, by exploring dialogue organization and task performance (O'Conaill, Whittaker & Wilbur, 1993; Doherty-Sneddon et al., 1997). These concerns were likewise relevant to conversation analysis (CA), which developed three main areas of enquiry, namely language-based, social-ethno-anthropological and mixed approaches to the study of 'online talk' (Paulus, Warren & Lester, 2016). Studies within the tradition of interactional sociology have shown the productivity of the application of *participatory frameworks* for the comprehension of media affordances (Hutchby, 2014), as derived from Goffman's model (Goffman, 1971, 1981). Among other pertinent interactional and sociolinguistic models, Goodwin's *cooperation model* illustrates the laminated organization of human action, whereby individuals cooperatively build action by putting together different semiotic signs that are part of a medium and, at the same time, shape how the medium itself works (Goodwin, 1989, 2000, 2013). Another take on the question is Scollon's *mediated discourse theory* (2001), which studies how practices are learnt and socialized by individuals and communities, with a focus on the *mediated nature of communication* (particularly so in the case of VMC), on background *sites of engagement* as entry points of observation in space and time, and *nexus of practice* as the node of social practices and mediated actions. Other examples from the social sciences include visual ethnography (Pink, 2007), pragmatics of computer-mediated communication (Herring, Stein & Virtanen, 2013), ethnomethodology and CA (Rintel, 2015), and other multidisciplinary work, such as the development of the visual data framework for the analysis of diverse video datasets, including mobile phone footage, body-worn cameras and video surveillance (Legewie & Nassauer, 2022).

Multimodal, sociosemiotic and translanguaging approaches have also developed systems to tackle the richly semiotic nature of VMC. The most current and relevant approaches here include multimodal visual analysis (van Leeuwen & Jewitt, 2001), multimodal interaction analysis (Norris, 2004), multimodal transcription and text analysis (Baldry, 2005; Baldry & Thibault, 2006, 2020) and systemic functional-multimodal discourse analysis (O'Halloran, 2004, 2008). A core methodological concern in this regard is the transcription and annotation of multimodal data to capture and reproduce the contribution of each semiotic resource, including, but not limited to, language to make meanings (see Flewitt et al., 2009).

In a recent chapter, Sindoni and Moschini (2021b: 205–6) summarized four major areas of interest connected with VMC in its synchronous and asynchronous formats, namely (1) the relationship between configurations of interpersonal communication; (2) affordances and constraints of technologies; (3) organization and distribution of turn-taking; and (4) their multimodal organization, not limited to language.

Thematically, task-oriented studies have been crucial for this domain's development, most specifically when investigating how tasks are interactionally organized in the workplace (Heath & Luff, 1992) and in educational contexts (Swan et al., 2008). In pedagogical scenarios, for example, Ho and Tai (2021) applied a multimodal and translanguaging lens to investigate how teachers use YouTube videos for role play in English-language online classes by multimodally drawing on different styles, registers and experiences and how educational materials were designed by teachers of English by orchestrating their multimodal and translingual repertoires. More recently, a systematic attempt to bring together multimodality and translanguaging in the context of asynchronous language learning on YouTube has been devised and applied to the 'street language learning' context by analysing how the vlogger Anming draws on her plurilinguistic, multisemiotic and multimodal repertoires to promote language learning 'on the move' (Sindoni & Ho, unpublished data).

Regardless of the theories and methods adopted, thematic studies have recurrently placed a focus on educational aspects, with reference to language learning and translingual practices, such as exploring the use of videos for English-language teaching (Kessler, Loewen & Trego, 2021), as well as on the multimodality of video-mediated interaction (VMI), for example analysing the influence of tasks on discourse strategies in virtual 3D settings (Shih, 2014) and on students' engagement with 360-degree videos through multimodal data analytics (Tan et al., 2020). Other studies have examined the management of personal media spaces in one-to-one and multiparty interactions as they emerge in specific media platforms, such as young people's use and understanding of spoken–written variation in Skype calls (Sindoni, 2011), affordances of online video game live streaming (Recktenwald, 2017), cross-modal engagements in Google Hangouts (Rosenbaun et al., 2016a, 2016b) and media ideologies in relation to FaceTime and WhatsApp (Busch & Sindoni, 2022).

The intrinsic, context and culture-dependent vitality of VMC transpires from the multiplicity of theories and methods used to make sense of, and learn from, the interactions conducted online in a wide range of settings well before the Covid-19 pandemic. Within this multiplicity of approaches, this Element specifically combines theories of multimodality and translanguaging. In Section 1.2, the benefits of selectively integrating theories and the empirical methods adopted in these two theoretical models are illustrated to show how their combination mutually invigorates and broadens their agenda.

1.2 Multimodality and Translanguaging: A Common Reformist Agenda

Video-mediated communication is inherently multimodal, like any other communicative event, but it is generally richer and, overall, more complex to follow and make sense of due to the intense and interlaced co-presence of semiotic resources, or modes, that contribute to overall meaning making. Multimodality has been defined as both a theory and a method to unravel such complexities by unpacking the resources that contribute to meaning making (Jewitt, 2014). Multimodality derives from the sociosemiotic model developed by Michael A. K. Halliday in the 1970s, who expanded the notion of text to include semiotic resources other than language:

> We can define text, in the simplest way perhaps, by saying that it is language that is functional. . . . So any instance of living language that is playing some part in a context of situation, we shall call it a text. *It may be either spoken or written, or indeed in any other medium of expression that we like to think of.* (Halliday, 1989: 10, my emphasis)

This idea was not certainly new, as it can be dated back to the well-known Saussurean conception of semiology as the science of signs (de Saussure, [1916] 2011). Nevertheless, Halliday accelerated an intellectual movement of semioticians and critical linguists, including Gunther Kress, Theo van

Leeuwen, Bob Hodge and the New London Group, who set out to account for the systems of regularities of semiotic resources and modes (the so-called grammars) other than language (see, for example, O'Toole, 1994; Kress & van Leeuwen, [1996] 2020). Particularly relevant insights for our context were presented in the manifesto by the New London Group (1996), who heralded the notion of *multiliteracies*. These were meant to overcome 'traditional language-based approaches' to learning, so as to challenge orthodox literacy pedagogy, which was firmly grounded on reading and writing practices connected to 'page-bound, official and standard forms of the *national language*' (1996: 61, my emphasis). They made the important point that literacy pedagogy had been designed as a project, 'restricted to *formalized, monolingual, monocultural*, and *rule-governed forms of language*' (1996: 61, my emphasis). The concept of national language, which had prevailed at that time in curriculum design, content and forms of assessment, needed to be challenged in that it projected a monolingual and monocultural context that was a myth rather than a reality. In response to the global communicative phenomena that had already started to gain momentum in the 1990s, their plan for pedagogical reform was proposed to account for the diversity of texts, discourses, languages and cultures that were circulating at the time.

An emphasis on visual 'language/s' amidst the rapid cha(lle)nges of modernity and an increased need to raise awareness about the multicultural and plurilinguistic repertoires of speakers was felt more acutely in the geographical areas where the New London Group was joining forces, namely the United States, Europe and Australia. They anticipated the development of a metalanguage of multiliteracies based on the concept of 'design', framed within a theory of discourse in which semiotic activities 'are *creative* application and combination of conventions (resources – Available Designs) that, in the process of Design, *transforms* at the same time it *reproduces* these conventions' (New London Group, 1996: 74, my emphasis).

In the New London Group authors' view, the Available Designs include the grammars of the other semiotic systems, such as language, film, gesture and photography. Hence, within the order of discourses, Available Designs take on different shapes, becoming styles, genres, voices, and so on. In other words, when speakers design texts, events and interactions, they draw on systems of sociolinguistic practice as well as on grammars. Crucially, the authors argued that 'the process of shaping emergent meaning involves re-presentation and recontextualization. This is never simply a repetition of Available Designs. Every moment of meaning involves the *transformation* of the available resources of meaning. Reading, seeing, and listening are all instances of Designing' (1996: 75, my emphasis). Hence, in their interpretation (and subsequent ones), meaning making can emerge out of Available Designs, or resources, that are never reproduced automatically by sign makers, but imply an act of *creative transformation* on their part.

Production of 'grammars' ensued. These described systems of meaning making as part of this much-needed treasure trove of multiliteracies. These grammars were intended to add a breath of epistemological fresh air to 'language-alone' models of literacy, for example with descriptions of regularities of different systems of meaning making, such as the built environment of displayed art (O'Toole, 1994), (mostly) still images (Kress & van Leeuwen, 2020), music (van Leeuwen, 1999), short films (Baldry & Thibault, 2006), mathematics (O'Halloran, 2006), document layout (Bateman, 2008) and three-dimensional texts (Ravelli & McMurtrie, 2015), to name but a few. Along with the development of these 'grammars' as models to act upon resources and empower the agency of the sign maker, the manifesto prompted the emergence of several pedagogical reformist agendas grounded on the intrinsic transformative nature of meaning making (Kress, 2000, 2003). Additionally, by resisting approaches that were exclusively focused on language as the sole resource to make meanings and to understand communication, multimodally oriented studies started to examine texts, events, performances or any other kind of artefacts (such as objects, toys and buildings) that could even not include any language at all. In this sense, the reformist project of multimodality was concerned with proving that communication went well beyond language and that linguistics needed to embrace a more far-reaching view and, at the same time, be informed by sociosemiotics.

The reformist agenda that lies at the core of the historical origins of multimodal and sociosemiotic studies can likewise be traced back to the earliest conceptualizations of the translanguaging project. Within one tradition, the term derives from the Welsh *trawsieithu* coined by Cen Williams (1994) and translated into English by Colin Baker in 2011 (see García & Li, 2014; García & Lin, 2016). It originally referred to bilingual students involved in the pedagogical practice of alternating English and Welsh in class activities, for example speaking in one language and writing in the other. Thanks to movements from various parts of the world advocating the pursuit of linguistic rights in the second half of the twentieth century, bilingualism and multilingualism started to be seen as political constructs. The development of translanguaging theories has been paramount in this paradigm shift. García explained this shift by contending that translanguaging is 'an approach to bilingualism that is centred not on languages as has been often the case, but on the practices of bilinguals that are readily observable' (2009: 44). In her view, translanguaging is a set of '*multiple discursive practices* in which bilinguals engage in order *to make sense of their bilingual worlds*' (2009: 45, emphasis in the original). In a similar vein, Creese and Blackledge (2010) challenge the 'two solitudes' assumption of bilingual education (see Cummins, 2008) and propose a model of 'flexible bilingualism' that places speakers at its centre, but which is not idealized and does not hold monoglossic beliefs about language. Other significant lines of enquiry are pursued by Canagarajah, who has highlighted the dual nature of translanguaging as a theory and as a practice (2013, 2020, 2022). Taking *monolingual orientation* (Canagarajah, 2013) as his point of departure, he developed the notion of *codemeshing*. This recognizes the fluid nature of communication and the hybridization of languages and varieties that become meshed with other symbolic systems, such as icons, emoticons or other graphical resources and modalities, including images, audio and video.

The reformist agenda is clearly foregrounded in Li's work. The dimensions of 'creativity' and 'transformation' resonate in Li's theoretical design of translanguaging as the act of seamlessly navigating through linguistic structures and systems across modalities, such as speaking, writing, signing and remembering, but at the same time transcending them (Li, 2011). Li draws attention to the transformation implicit in what he defines as a 'translanguaging space':

> The act of translanguaging then is *transformative* in nature; it creates a social space for the multilingual language user by bringing together different dimensions of their personal history, experience and environment, their attitude, belief and ideology, their cognitive and physical capacity into one coordinated and meaningful performance, and making it into a lived experience. I call this space '*translanguaging space*', a space for the act of translanguaging as well as a space created through translanguaging. (Li, 2011: 1223, my emphasis)

Li's approach mirrors the general translanguaging project to 'decolonize' linguistics from the 'lingual bias' found in much second language acquisition research, including that concerned with bilingualism and multilingualism (Block, 2014). The 'lingual bias' equates overall communication with language properties (e.g., phonology, morphology, syntax, lexis), thus disregarding questions of pragmatic, intercultural and learning dimensions and not addressing 'embodiment and multimodality as a broadened semiotically based way of looking at what people do when they interact' (Block, 2014: 56). This decolonizing project, however, is organized around a focus other than the one identified in multimodal studies. Translanguaging has been broadly designed as the attempt to resist monoglossic views that posit the existence of abstract linguistic structures in separate areas of bilingual and multilingual speakers' brains. On the theoretical level, the different languages and varieties started to be conceptualized, and consequently described, as multifaceted linguistic repertoires that had only been *heuristically* and *ideologically* named as 'distinct' languages. The clear-cut boundaries that distinguished one language or variety from another in fact reflected normative, prescriptive and top-down approaches within an underlying political agenda. The different linguistic repertoires could, and indeed should, be represented as plurilinguistic continua interlaced with the personal, individual, social and cultural life trajectories of language users. The names of languages are therefore political constructs rather than intrinsically linguistic descriptive labels. The names of languages are outward oriented rather than inward oriented.

Against these deterministic views, Li proposed to repurpose the theoretical agenda of (applied) linguistics by formulating the paradigm-shifting claim that language is 'a multilingual, multisemiotic, multisensory, and multimodal resource for sense- and meaning-making' (Li, 2018: 22). This intellectual endeavour was framed around one focus that still today foregrounds language analyses (mostly, but not exclusively within educational scenarios), with a sensitivity to multilingual and plurilingual contexts, as well as pragmatic, intercultural and sociosemiotic realities (Zhu, Li & Jankowicz-Pytel, 2020). Meaning making, within translanguaging perspectives, is understood as *a semiotic act and choice* in ways that run parallel to those theorized in multimodality. However, while translanguaging theories are primarily focused on examining how language users draw on their plurilinguistic and multisemiotic repertoires to make and exchange meanings, multimodality may analyse events, practices and artefacts that have no language whatsoever included.

Even though multimodal and translanguaging theories come from different pedagogical, sociosemiotic and linguistic research traditions and directions, they share a profoundly reformist agenda that puts speakers – wherever their life worlds and trajectories are – at the core of meaning making, as they are immersed in ever-evolving creative and transformative practices. If the New London Group manifesto and ensuing multimodal and pedagogical theories contested the automatic primacy assigned to monolithic literacy pedagogies (Cope & Kalantzis, 2021), translanguaging, as a 'practical theory of language' (Li, 2018), reconceptualizes language as broader than a phonetic, lexical, grammatical and syntactical complex of structures so as to incorporate its multilingual, multisemiotic, multisensory and multimodal components (Li, 2018: 22).

While resisting approaches that prioritize language and adopt monoglossic views, both multimodality and translanguaging theories, in their multiple strands, recognize that 'human languaging activity is radically heterogeneous and involves the interaction of processes on many different time-scales, including neural, bodily, situational, social, and cultural processes and events'

(Thibault, 2017: 76). These combined approaches to communication provide a
fully fledged model that reflects the need to incorporate the multilinguistic and
multisemiotic repertoires of speakers, in order to capture the complexities of
contemporary communication in the classroom and beyond (Zhu, Li &
Jankowicz-Pytel, 2020) in its analysis and description. Repertoires are richly
interlaced ensembles of available resources and modes that speakers orchestrate
to communicate in a variety of contexts, practices and across a range of forms of
embodied and/or disembodied configurations that make meanings and cause
them to be circulated. By way of summary, multimodality and translanguaging
have distinct theories, methodologies, research foci and different preferential
objects of study. Consistent with their historical (and parallel) developments
that addressed two major concerns in linguistics – logocentrism in multimodality versus monoglossic ethnocentrism in translanguaging – these two theories
are highly compatible and can contribute to increasing awareness about how
communication works in plurilingual, multisemiotic and multimodal scenarios,
with both *embodied* and *disembodied resources* for meaning making.

1.3 An Overview of This Element

Building on the arguments provided in the previous sections, this Element
begins by assuming that multimodality and translanguaging can reciprocally
benefit from each other. In what follows, the resources and modes of VMIs will
be analysed by combining the insights and methodologies of multimodality and
translanguaging. The overarching aim of this Element is therefore to show how
these two theories and methodologies can be complementary to unpack communicative events, be they mediated or not. In subsequent sections, multimodality and translanguaging will not be merged or incorporated into one another.
They will be selectively used to illustrate the two models in action in the context
of VMC instead.

The broad theoretical question that will be addressed in this Element deals
with how multimodality and translanguaging can work in partnership to understand the meaning making in VMC and beyond. The underlying assumption is
that both share a common reformist agenda that underpins their models. This
reformist agenda is neither abstract nor vague and encapsulates two principles
that will be shown in action. The first multimodal principle is that communication goes beyond the verbal and that the verbal can in fact be missing without
compromising successful communication. The second translanguaging principle is that the labels of languages and varieties (e.g., English, Tagalog,
Spanish, Sicilian or Mandarin Chinese) are political constructs and that what
language users do with languages (and/or with any other semiotic resource or

mode) cannot be pinned down by clear-cut linguistic taxonomies that do not account for personal and community life trajectories or for specific pragmatic or functional goals.

This Element will systematically map the resources that come into play in VMC by accounting for the translinguistic/plurilinguistic, multisemiotic and multicultural repertoires of speakers as they perceive and make sense of them. The *embodied resources* include speech, gaze, proxemics and kinesics patterns, while *disembodied resources* incorporate writing and images, among others (Sindoni, 2013), in ways that are made salient and meaningful by participants in situated contexts.

In Section 2, the resource of language will be unpacked in the typical multimodal conceptualization of *mode* (or resource), that is, more specifically, in the configuration of *speech* and *writing* rather than that of language *tout court*. Kress defined mode as a 'socially shaped and culturally given resource for making meaning' (Kress, 2009: 54), thus carrying 'the discernible regularities of social occasions, event and hence a certain stability' (Kress, 2010: 8). He argued that common instances of modes are '*speech; still image; moving image; writing; gesture; music; 3D models; action; colour*' (Kress, 2010: 28, emphasis in the original). Kress himself problematized the speech/writing labelling that, in his view, was not so clear-cut if placed in a cultural context. To corroborate his problematization of the speech/writing categorization, he mentioned as examples the different script systems for writing and the distinction between tone languages and intonation languages for speech (Kress, 2010). However, even within these caveats, language cannot be semiotically unpacked into the categories of speech and writing alone. This semiotic categorization is mostly unsatisfactory, and for a number of reasons. Viewing language as a resource only in its spoken and written components is in fact certainly highly reductionist. The question of how different languages and varieties can *semiotically* influence and shape communication is mostly left underexplored in multimodal research (Kress and van Leeuwen, 2001; Kress, 2009, 2010). Even though several multimodal studies deal with translingual and intercultural case studies, those languages and varieties are not conceptualized as semiotically different, but rather as intrinsically similar languaging variants. This Element wishes to draw attention to the distinct ontologies of languages and varieties in the moment they are used in context. These distinct ontologies incorporate distinct but compatible forms of language variation (be they from speech to writing or from one language to another one) as triggers of *creativity* and *transformation*, along the lines indicated by Li (2011).

The case studies in Section 2 will illustrate how users make sense of *alternations* between speech and writing, defined as *mode-switching* (i.e., alternation of speech and writing within the same communicative event). These will be used as a frame to introduce Section 3, which presents other forms of alternations, namely those between and across different languages and varieties, to examine similar patterns of meaning making, as well as differences. Rather than forcing interpretative evaluations on the patterns emerging from the video samples and interviews, the analyses will be more focused on showing participants' reflections on their and others' video interactions, along with their diverse degrees of metapragmatic awareness.

In Section 4 and 5, other patterns of meaning making in VMC will be illustrated, namely the use of gaze in its manifold configurations in video-mediated environments (e.g., lack of mutual gaze, practice of self-looking), as well as rearrangements of personal space and social distance (what will be defined as 'staged proxemics' in Section 5) and bodily presence, as mainly instantiated in head, hand and torso movements in the video frame.

Within these scenarios, the complex notion of 'intercultural communication' will be tackled as perceived and made sense of by individuals. It is a wide, interdisciplinary and multifaceted area and a discussion of its many interlaced components goes beyond the scope of this Element. When explicitly mentioned, intercultural communication will be identified here as 'concerned with how individuals, in order to achieve their communication goals, negotiate cultural or linguistic differences which may be perceived relevant by at least one party in the interaction' (Zhu, 2019: 2010). The suggestion to problematize 'the notion of cultural identities' and emphasize 'the *emergent, discursive* and *inter* nature of interactions' (Zhu, 2013: 9, emphasis in the original) will be taken up in the analyses of discourse practices of learners and research participants.

1.4 A Methodological Note on Datasets

The subsequent sections selectively draw on several datasets used to illustrate examples of how resources are used in VMIs that were collected over a ten-year time span. This video corpus comprises over 900 hours of recorded interactions in a wide variety of contexts, such as educational settings, leisure and affinity spaces, and taken from a range of platforms, including one-to-one (e.g., Skype and FaceTime) and multiparty (e.g., Camfrog). All the data has been collected ethically, that is, always informing participants of research purposes and distributing informed consent forms. Names have been changed when possible, that is, when it did not involve changing the original students' transcriptions, which are all reproduced here unedited.

A small sample of this larger dataset includes recorded video interactions of university learners in two research projects, namely: (1) twenty-one video interactions from the European-funded project EU-MaDE4LL, European Multimodal and Digital Education for Language Learning (2016–19), (2) twenty-four from the Italian national project MoM, Multimodality on the Move (2014–15) and (3) thirty-two VMIs from the VIDEO dataset ('Video Interactions in Digital EnvirOnments') that I obtained from my research on these topics and from a variety of participants, giving a total of seventy-seven VMIs in one-to-one contexts.

The video data from the first two research projects was obtained in a controlled environment and under similar conditions. The VMIs were recorded for research purposes in university contexts and by students who had been informed beforehand of the projects' learning objectives. Both projects had common core classes taught by five researchers on five different digital texts,[1] with multimodality, digital literacies and English as the language of intercultural communication as the three pedagogical milestones. Core courses for undergraduate and postgraduate students were delivered by the researchers in their home universities. All the researchers then visited the other universities to deliver their workshops on the digital text in which they were experts. I taught the workshop on VMIs in all the classes involved in both projects (nine altogether, four undergraduate and five postgraduate), in relation to personal and professional contexts (e.g., video conversations and job interviews).

The final assignment for the students who had chosen VMIs as the digital text for end-of-course formal submission consisted of four tasks: (1) a recording of a video call with a friend or with another student; (2) a multimodal transcription of a maximum of three minutes of interaction on a pre-filled grid, meant to unpack all the multimodal resources involved; (3) a written analysis of c. 3,000 words that explained how learners had gone about the multimodal transcription and how it had helped them to make sense of the overall interaction; (4) a peer-assessment grid about another student's transcription and written analysis. All peer-assessment tasks involved evaluation of the same digital text type, so that learners had the chance to assess the same tasks they had already carried out at an earlier stage of the project. These materials amount to a total of 192 university students' digital and multimodal productions only for VMIs.[2]

---

[1] The researchers in the MoM project, with taught digital texts in brackets, were: Elisabetta Adami (blogs), Ilaria Moschini (fanvids), Sandra Petroni ('about us' webpages) and Maria Grazia Sindoni (VMIs). The researchers in the EU-MaDE4LL project were the same with the addition of Carmen D. Maier (promotional videos).

[2] Details about the overall materials of the project can be found in the final outcome of the project, namely the CFRIDiL https://www.eumade4ll.eu/wp-content/uploads/2020/02/cfridil-frame work-linked-fin1.pdf.

The Peer Assessment Form and the Teacher Assessment Form, which have been developed within the EU-MaDE4LL project, are supplementary materials to this Element and can be freely downloaded, adapted and reused in the classroom. The Guidelines for Classroom Activities at university level for the module on VMIs are also provided in this Element.[3]

Excerpts of short video conversations between university students complemented by their own multimodal transcriptions and annotations are selectively inserted in the sections to show how conversations can be linearly analysed and how the students' media, multilingual and multimodal ideologies (Gershon, 2010a and 2010b) emerge from transcription and annotation tasks. These provide insights into their perceptions, understanding and sense making of translinguistic and semiotic resources (Busch, 2018; Busch & Sindoni, 2022). All the EU-MaDE4LL teaching and learning materials and content have been used to develop the *Common Framework of Reference for Intercultural Digital Literacies* (Sindoni et al., 2019).

2 Familiar, Reconfigured and Emergent Uses of Speech and Writing

Synchronous and real-time VMC *seems* to replicate the conversational dynamics of face-to-face conversations. People talk following more or less the same rules that apply in face-to-face settings, such as managing turn-taking, asking for and giving the floor, and using self-correction and any other repair strategy to keep interaction flowing smoothly. At least to a certain extent, they can likewise use all the 'multimodal' dimensions of gaze as conversational facilitators, make use of body movements and adopt forms of social distance as in real-life contexts, albeit with all the provisos discussed in more detail in the following sections. Broadly speaking with regard to speech, gaze, body movements and positions, VMC seems to differ from face-to-face interactions only from a technological standpoint. This implies, in its most basic definition, the use of mediational means, for example, a *screen*, either from a desktop or mobile device, to allow communication *and* simulate presence, by means of an internet connection. However, the exceptional contingencies of the pandemic have underscored the challenges and problems faced by its exponentially larger number of users, as mentioned in Section 1. As shown by a growing number of studies, these issues cannot be explained merely as a technological issue – or as a lack of digital skills. This section explores how these 'familiar' resources deployed in VMC are in fact 'reconfigured'.

---

[3] The Peer Assessment Form, Teacher Assessment Form and the Guidelines for Classroom Activities are available from the following link: www.cambridge.org/Sindoni.

The title of this section paraphrases an expression coined by Susan C. Herring at the Georgetown University Round Table in 2010 (Herring, 2012) and alludes to the familiar uses of speech and writing in digital environments, as well as the modified and restructured patterns that this Element aims to discuss in comparison with face-to-face contexts.

Synchronous video calls, as already mentioned, are two-way interactions where two or more participants can converse in real time. Examples include: (1) virtual meetings on Skype, Microsoft Teams, Google Meet, WebEx and other telecommunication platforms; (2) live online classes via video-conferencing technologies; (3) open discussion sessions in workplace settings; (4) live events, webinars and communication produced with video-conferencing software and (5) Slack chats, threaded discussions, VOIP and video calls when participants are engaging in real time (Panopto, 2022). While VMC can be loosely differentiated into distinct configurations, as shown in Table 1, common conversational and interactional dynamics can be observed in all these forms of mediated communication.

Table 1 Types of synchronous VMC.

Types of synchronous VMC	Most prominent features	Format
1. Video calls	Two participants live stream, communicating using a video through landline, mobile or internet network.	One-to-one
2. Video conferencing	The number of participants is greater than two, but they are not necessarily all shown on screen. However, a grid may be shown with a pre-set number of screens that can be shown simultaneously.	Internal/team meetings External/all-hands meetings
3. Telepresence	A more sophisticated form of VMC where a real setting is simulated so that each participant seems to be sitting next to each other.	Internal/team meetings External/all-hands meetings

Section 2.1 compares real-time face-to-face and video-mediated events with a focus on the distinct uses of speech, which is the most widely used resource, at least in a typical or generic video call. Some examples of medium-specific uses of writing in VMC are then presented and discussed.

2.1 Speech and Writing: Is This Still a Useful Distinction?

Whatever their communicative function may be, synchronous and spontaneous spoken face-to-face interaction displays recurring conversational planning and structuring patterns that can be broadly summarized as: (1) shared co-presence of participants; (2) common situational context; (3) involvement strategies; (4) other-paced dynamics, and (5) features typical of spontaneous interaction, such as repetition, pauses, hesitations, self-corrections, use of discourse markers (Schiffrin, 1986), rephrasing, and so on (Sindoni, 2013, see also Laver, 1975), along with other non-verbal features, such as gaze distribution, social distance (Hall, 1966) and body movement organization (i.e., kinesics, see, e.g., Scheflen, 1964 and Ekman & Friesen, 1969), or halfway strategies spanning verbal and non-verbal features, such as prosodic and intonational modelling.

As argued by Kress (2003), the association between mode and medium used to be more straightforward before the advent of the digital era, for example writing used to be immediately associated with a book or with book-like features, but today this association no longer holds. Writing displays the features of oral language in a number of different contexts, being used for spontaneous, non-editable, redundant and non-standard communication in digital settings (Baron, 2000). VMIs are one interactional digital scenario where the distinction between spoken and written discourse becomes blurred and fuzzy (Sindoni, 2013). The daily use of social media, email writing, smartphone use, and interconnected devices and platforms displays how has this distinction been further blurred. Speech is still interactional and makes use of involving and cooperative strategies, but writing has been consistently used in ways that can be compared to speech. The advent of digital writing has normalized informality, repetitions, spontaneity and the quick decay of anything written. Writing is used for social media posts and comments and in instant messaging apps, and has taken many unprecedented forms. Against the backdrop of the digital conversational world, writing has perhaps never been less permanent than before in the history of human communication. Hence the question as to whether the distinction between speech and writing still needs to be made has been raised.

Several multimodal researchers prefer the distinction of speech and writing rather than the more abstract definition of language. As made explicit in their textbook, Jewitt, Bezemer and O'Halloran (2016: 15) claim that 'by "language" we mean speech and writing'. Kress provides a clear explanation for this preference. He argues that it would be a hard task to find principles of coherence for different features in speech (e.g., what pitch variation has in common with lexis, or what connects levels of energy, such as loudness and softness, with syntax). It would be likewise hard to find principles of coherence for disparate sets of features in writing, such as what fonts have in common with lexis or orthography with syntax (Kress, 2010). He then provides the following argument:

> Joining all these features under one label, of *speech* or of *writing*, shows one problem. But collapsing speech and writing with their entirely different materiality in one category, thereby joining and blurring over the distinct logics of time and space, of sequence and simultaneity, exposes the implausibility of a mode called 'language'. It is difficult to see what principles of coherence might serve to unify all these features. So I take *speech* and *writing* to be distinct modes (Kress, 2010: 86, emphasis in the original).

More recently, Diamantopoulou and Ørevik published a volume on multimodality in English-language learning scenarios, adopting a transnational and 'international outlook', as they put it (2022: 4). Their description of 'mode' follows the tradition of multimodal social semiotics: 'a culturally shaped semiotic resource, such as writing, speech, movement, gesture, and gaze' (Diamantopoulou & Ørevik, 2022: 9), hence with no explicit reference to if and how diverse translingual practices may impact on meaning making. In their attempt to delineate the principles of a general semiotics, Bezemer and Kress (2016) had made the point that this theory should identify which semiotic principles are shared and how these principles are differently realized in each mode (as explained in Jewitt, Bezemer & O'Halloran, 2016). This interest in what is common and what is different, what the gains and losses are in the use of each mode, and which affordances can activate or silence meaning potential is a central concern for multimodal studies (Kress, 2005). However, the question of whether drawing from plurilinguistic repertoires can be considered only in terms of speech and writing is left underexplored.

Translanguaging theories likewise show interest in the concepts of the modes of speech and writing as descriptive for language use. For example, Baynham and Lee revisit the work of the linguist Whorf and argue that 'every language has its affordances, enabling some ways of thinking and disabling others. . . . It is perhaps even more obvious that different modes (spoken/written/visual/gestural/embodied) have different affordances' (Baynham & Lee, 2019: 29). With this claim, they connect modes with affordances and seem to adhere to the general semiotic principle of the speech/writing dyad as accounting for language affordances (or materiality).

If it is certainly true that all languages and varieties are sign systems (i.e., made up of modes to make meanings), it is questionable whether the dyad of speech and writing is satisfactory to describe all forms of alternation, meshing, mixing across modes, languages and varieties. This question will be taken up further in Section 3.

In this section, speech and writing will be used as heuristic categories suitable for describing the distinct ways of making meaning by means of their different affordances (i.e., what one can do and cannot do with them) and by means of the meaning making of their medium-specific alternations in VMC. Speech and writing in fact follow different coherence principles; they activate and silence different affordances. In VMI, the readily available affordance of writing a message in the text chat box makes its use far more frequent than could be found in face-to-face encounters. The use of writing in offline contexts cannot be excluded a priori, in cases such as passing a written note to another person or sending a private text message by WhatsApp or any other instant message platform, but the exchange of written messages in VMI is much more frequent and normalized (Bateman et al., unpublished data; Sindoni, 2011, 2013, 2019).

Section 2.2 explores these VMI-specific patterns in more detail.

2.2 Speech and Writing in VMC

Unlike face-to-face conversations, which typically rely heavily on speech to make and exchange meanings, video conversations allow for the incorporation of written turns that can be inserted in the chat box of the most common video platforms (Sindoni et al., 2019; Sindoni, Adami, Karatza, Moschini et al., 2021; Sindoni, Adami, Moschini, Petroni & Karatza, 2021). These written comments can be employed for a variety of reasons, ranging from technical issues, for example when speakers cannot hear each other or need to fill in gaps over some time lag, to pragmatic and cultural uses, such as communicating more personal contents (e.g., in one-to-one contexts) or as a face-saving strategy, with writing perceived as a 'less embarrassing' and 'less compromising' resource when potentially sensitive subjects are touched on (Sindoni, 2012, 2014). I have labelled this medium-specific pattern as *mode-switching*, alluding to the spontaneous alternation of speech and writing within the same communicative video exchange (Sindoni, 2011). Examples taken from video-based interactions document different pragmatic and cultural practices, useful for unveiling speakers' language and media ideologies (Busch, 2018; Gershon, 2010b; Li & Zhu, 2013), as well as participatory engagements, cross-model exchanges

(Rosenbaun et al., 2016a, 2016b) and media asymmetries (Heath & Luff, 1992). Starting from heuristically categorizing several forms of mode-switching (e.g., *self-initiated* versus *other-initiated*), other patterns of speech-writing variation are mentioned in this Element, with reference to culture, context, setting and media affordances (Gibson, 1986 [1979]). These patterns are analysed to explore how these variables influence the way in which speech and writing are alternated in video-mediated environments.

This toolkit is meant to encourage awareness about how modes and media facilitate communication in some circumstances (for example, the possibility of alternating speech and writing by keeping the text chat box open to allow for multiple conversation floors), but hinder mutual intelligibility if resources are not distributed meaningfully and/or evenly (for example, if teachers leave these channels open haphazardly or if learners do not know how to avoid overlapping in spoken/written modes). The two main research questions dealt with in Section 2.3 are:

- RQ1: What are the main communicative functions of mode-switching in video conversations?
- RQ2: How do speakers take advantage of media affordances in video-conferencing platforms? How do they switch from speech to writing and vice versa and to what end?

2.3 Speech, Writing and Mode-Switching in VMC

The communicative feature that will be the focus of this section is specific to VMC, but is not related to any particular platform as all client systems supporting synchronous and video-based exchanges allow users to decide which channel can be used. As already anticipated, using writing in spoken interaction is certainly feasible in face-to-face scenarios, such as giving someone a slip of paper while talking, or even writing on the blackboard while speaking in a classroom context. However, the patterns of regularities that characterize the alternation between speech and writing in VMIs allow systematic and empirical descriptions.

A first basic difference has to do with media affordances, and in particular with the number of people involved in communication. One-to-many means that one participant broadcasts live, while the others are not connected with each other. This type of VMI will not be dealt with in this Element, as no direct and ongoing interaction is entailed. However, as both involve a live exchange between users, the distinctions between many-to-many and one-to-one interactions are dealt with in the following two sub-sections.

2.3.1 Many-to-Many VMIs, or Multiuser Video Chat

Many-to-many VMIs, as the label suggests, are meetings that include multiple users found in professional contexts, such as business meetings and educational settings, including online video classes, which, despite their widespread use during the Covid-19 pandemic, were already a well-established aspect of remote learning contexts, whose features are defined and investigated in this section with reference to a multiparty video platform.

From 2011 to 2013, I analysed several hours of video interactions in a Camfrog room named *SpeakEnglish* for people interested in conversations in English. Camfrog is a video-based online community for up to one thousand users in a single room. Media affordances of this platform allow the visualization of participants' screens, their roles and status, and of a foregrounded text chat box used to post comments and add multimodal materials, such as emoticons, emojis, virtual gifts, and much more besides. The platform's configuration clearly foregrounds the text chat box's central position. This has a highly salient visual status, as only *one* person can speak at a time.

Over a two-year time span, I interviewed about one hundred participants. My interviews were based on the observation of their uses of the two channels of communication, namely how they modulated their uses of speech and writing and their degree of awareness in reflecting on their use with guided questions (see Sindoni, 2011, 2013). Some of the questions are reported in the infographic reproduced in Figure 1.

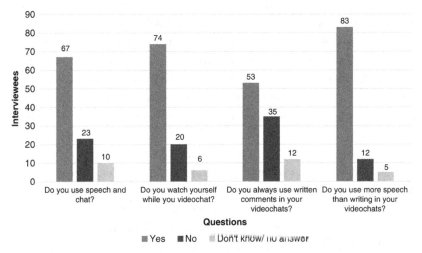

Figure 1 Results of interviews (2011–13).

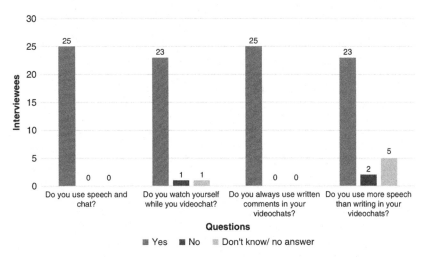

Figure 2 Results of interviews (2020–22).

I conducted another set of unstructured interviews in 2020–22 with a much smaller number of users (twenty-five), including, among others, Camfrog users, to acquire a broader understanding of how the communicative scenario had been changing, if at all. I repeated the same questions, but with different and fewer interviewees, as reproduced in the infographic in Figure 2, during the Covid-19 outbreak and beyond (years 2020–22).

All interviewees, both from the first (2011–13) and second batch (2020–22) of interviews, claimed that the primary reason for using the text chat box was to hold parallel floors of conversations. The wording of their responses varied greatly, but this mode-switching, in both *self-initiated* and *other-initiated* (i.e., prompted by other users) forms, was clearly identified and motivated by participants. Some excerpts of my more recent interviews are reproduced here:

Excerpt 1: I use it to send my comments. Yes, these comments. When other people are speaking, yes, I want just to say something or comment with some little emoji or something, yes, I write there.

Excerpt 2: I don't speak often. Yes, I prefer the. Erm … yes, I send IM [instant messages]. Sometimes I IM only one user, if I don't want all to see. Yeah, I can IM from my list. But I prefer pause my video and see what's going on there. And IM now and then.

Parallel conversation floors are also kept in the public chat and in the private instant message channel, as specified by one user in Excerpt 2. An external user would encounter problems to know how these multiple floors of conversations

Figure 3 A snapshot of a conversation on a multiparty video room (date: 3 December 2022).

develop across the spoken and written channels, and this is especially true when translanguaging occurs. In these platforms, translingual practices are interspersed within these multi-layered conversations where interlocutors come and go very quickly. An example is reproduced in Figure 3.

As Figure 3 shows, a decontextualized instance of the written conversation is extremely complex to decode – not so much because of the absence of audio at this point,[4] but rather because several interlaced conversations were being conducted in the written channel. No cooperative conversation principle seems to be at work, at least not when reading the messages sequentially. Semiotic resources, such as colour, font, hyperlinks and platform codes (such as stars and crowns) are all employed to convey additional meanings. With reference to language, the multiple channels, in speech and in writing, are employed by users to enhance and maximize their participation and engagement with the others. When asked about their translingual practices, one user replied:

Excerpt 3: I use Thai when I want that only [another user's nickname] understands.

---

[4] The audio has not been reproduced here as it was mostly unrelated to the content discussed in the written thread, with the exception of messages by Jad_27 and zarda_paan, who were also speaking over the audio channel about their physical appearance and their general attitudes and preferences.

When questioned about how he could be sure that no one in the chatroom spoke Thai, considering the ease of access and constant fluctuation of people in the room, he replied:

Excerpt 4: Ahah. Right. Ah. But [another user's nickname] knows that . . . and she knows that I'm talking to her. Or. I don't care, I can also IM her.

In Excerpt 4, the informant recognizes the fact that Camfrog has not been designed to have full and continuous knowledge of who is in the room at any moment in time. Nonetheless, he prefers to switch to Thai when addressing another user so that he is sure that she will appreciate the specific nuances of meaning and the forms of direct address. This excerpt provides evidence that translingual practices are not mere functional activities, but are rather interpersonal and performative. As indicated by the informant, he could have sent an instant message (IM) and have a private conversation in Thai, but he chose not to do so. In this light, translingual performances are fully meaning making in that they show intentionality, as well as semiotic (implicit) awareness. More details on these translingual practices will be further provided in Section 3.

As these examples show, multiuser video-conferencing software is likely to be perceived by external users as highly chaotic. Any stretch of conversation taken from the rooms that I have studied over the years is complex to decode, irrespective of its written, audio or shared video materials. The participants, however, seem to be at ease with this format and when asked whether they have ever experienced problems in making sense of what was happening in their video chats, they were almost unanimous in confirming their comprehension, as shown in Excerpts 5 and 6:

Excerpt 5: Yes . . . erm . . . yeah, you know, maybe it's you, no, we all see what's going on in here. You follow your conversation, right? And yes, you don't pay attention to what other people are saying, you only follow what your friends say, or other people . . .

Excerpt 6: Yes, I always understand what's going on. It's easier when you get the hang of it. Not such a big deal.

These examples show that the participants identified how expert users can manage multiple conversations by simply ignoring what is not relevant to them. It is as if a sort of 'selective attention' is activated to silence all the conversational noise. The participants generally agreed that platform newbies may experience serious miscommunication, but that as soon as time spent on the platform increases, the sense of conversational chaos rapidly disappears. The degree of confidence rises with experience and time spent on the platform, as self-assessed by participants. All of them claimed that being able to flip between spoken and written channels was key to successful communication. As one put it:

Excerpt 7: All you need to know is when you can talk and use the audio, when you can IM, when you can DM someone. Here we know which we can use, don't we?

However, not every multiparty video conversation needs a degree of expert knowledge as does Camfrog or similar video-based platforms. In educational contexts, for example, platforms, such as Microsoft Teams, Zoom or Google Meet, allow a more patterned and systematic organization of turn-taking across the spoken and written channels. The chat can be managed with options such as snoozing or turning off chat bubbles. These settings require a more disciplined and coordinated way of organizing VMIs. Communication is organized hierarchically, for example, when a teacher uses the video-mediated platform as a virtual classroom, thus keeping the floor for longer periods, and being the administrator of all students' turns.

The participants taking part in professional and educational VMIs and interviewed between 2020 and 2022 claimed that if there were a 'main' speaker,[5] such as a teacher, a lecturer, a team leader or any other person in charge of conveying the main content, or to satisfy the meeting's communicative purpose, they would use chats only to greet the others, to ask questions and to thank the 'main' speaker and/or the others. One informant remarked that the written chat is most likely to be used for greeting and thanking other people, and in much more explicit ways than is the case in face-to-face encounters.

In these contexts, speech is still the most foregrounded resource, the one that allows a face-to-face situation to be replicated. Writing is mostly considered as a corollary resource, used to greet the other discourse partners, ask questions without interrupting, thank and congratulate the speaker, and to signal technical issues. When asked about if and why they felt the need to greet and thank, most admitted that they tended to greet and thank *verbally* more than they would have done in presence because:

Excerpt 8: I want that the others feel my presence somehow. Also because I don't want to turn my webcam on, so if I don't say hi no-one will know I am there. I say that I'm there. And I like when other people reply or put a like on my post.

Excerpt 9: I write 'thank you' because I can't give a round of applause. I know we can click on the 'clapping hands' icon, but it doesn't work. I miss the cheering and involvement that we used to have in person. So I write these

---

[5] Fifty-seven participants took part in this specific part of the research.

things in the chat. Like 'thank you,' 'hi everyone', 'lovely to see you all' and stuff like this.

In other cases, such as those exemplified in Excerpt 10, participants explained that the written channel was used to address technical issues and signal media-related actions, such as logging in and out. These written 'justifications' are forms of polite addresses to the other participants afforded by the medium that allows for a secondary floor of communication (for example, when the video or audio channel does not work) or for the avoidance of unwanted interruptions.

Excerpt 10: Excuse me, I can't hear you, I have to log out and then get in again. Sorry.

In classroom contexts, students are likely to use the written chat as a substitute for speaking or for all other non-verbal behaviour indicating comprehension, agreement or following the arguments (such as nodding or looking at the teacher in real-life settings). When asked about their written chat use, all the students interviewed confirmed that their use of the written chat was a substitute for 'raising hands' in the classroom, or any other visual interactional cue asking for the floor without interrupting the teacher. I interviewed twenty-five students who used emojis to accompany their written comments. They argued that their function was mostly to express engagement and a constructive attitude. An example of this answer can be found in Excerpt 11:

Excerpt 11: Ok, I've never thought about it, but I guess I use them to be friendly. Yes, mm mm, to add some extra meaning, meanings, yes, to say that I was happy with it, yes, to be friendly.

They also argued that they merely replicated their use of emojis from other instant messaging apps, such as WhatsApp, and emails. However, they understood that the communication was asymmetrical because it occurred within a university context. They thus limited their emojis to only using the most neutral, such as the smiling face or the 'thumbs up' emoji. Coincidentally, all the students who used emojis engaged in the highest number of interactions, both in spoken and written channels. When questioned about the use of this emoji, students generally identified it as a resource to confirm attention or signal comprehension:

Excerpt 12: I used thumbs up on Teams basically to say 'yes, I got it'.

In both multiparty interactions for leisure time and for educational and/or professional settings, participants consistently use the written channel. In the former context, the communicative functions include holding parallel floors of conversation when multiple floors are activated by many speakers in symmetrical situations (that is, when there is no 'main' speaker, but all have equal status for claiming and keeping the floor). Additionally, the channel may be kept open for one specific speaker or a small group of speakers. In the latter context, the written channel is recognized as a supplementary feed for extra input.

As is to be expected, the use of multimodal resources is richer and freer in symmetrical communicative events and with no professional or educational agenda involved. Formal situations, conversely, prompt a more restrained use of multimodal contents, such as using 'neutral' emojis, uploading files and sending educational or professional materials.

2.3.2 One-to-One VMIs, or Personal Video Interactions

Video-conferencing systems usually allow chatting with one or more people, even though, as discussed in Section 2.3.1, some platforms were specifically designed for leisure group activities, whereas others, such as Zoom, Teams and Meet, are corporate oriented and adopted by several types of institutions, including schools, colleges and universities. The nature of one-to-one meetings can be either professional (e.g., one-to-one business meetings, remote office hours between students and teachers/professors, job interviews) or personal.

The MoM and EU-MaDE4LL datasets contain comparable data but with the important caveat that students (or at least approximately half of the people involved)[6] *were* a priori *aware* of the communicative events they were asked to analyse, such as mode-switching. Participants involved by the students in the recorded video calls, however, only had information about the research purposes, but were not given specific details as they were not relevant to them. The Information Sheet for this task can be downloaded here www.cambridge.org/Sindoni for inspection and re-use.

The transcriptions revealed many insights into their language and media ideologies, detailed in this and following sections. The VIDEO dataset, conversely, can be defined as *completely spontaneous* as it only includes videos submitted by voluntary members (with whom I have no teacher–student relationship) and it is only *ex post* (i.e., recorded for other unspecified reasons and then submitted for analysis).

Figure 4 and Table 2, respectively, summarize reasons given by a group of participants on why they mode-switched and explanations for these reasons (years 2011–13).

---

[6] Some students involved friends for their recording or submitted pre-recorded video interviews. All these secondary participants (as I defined them in Sindoni, 2019) were not aware of the interactional dynamics that were under study, so they may be assumed to be less self-conscious and more spontaneous.

Table 2 Reasons why users mode-switched (adapted from Sindoni, 2013).

Secrecy	Do not want to be heard/tell a secret, especially if someone who is not part of the conversation is in the room.
Intimacy	Communicate intimate feelings (e.g., love, friendship, affiliation, etc.) or express face-threatening feelings (embarrassment, shame, taboos, etc.).
Fun/Kidding	Add visual (e.g., through the use of emoticons) or expressive (e.g., through swear words) content.
Referential	Give precise information (e.g., addresses, telephone numbers, names, references, etc.).
Other	Not well aware about when and why they resort to written comments.

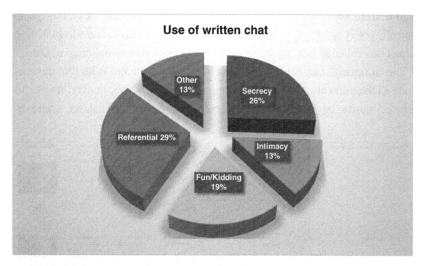

Figure 4 Percentage of reasons provided by users for mode-switching.

Despite variations relating to context and communicative purposes, this data may still prove useful to explain these occurrences. One strikingly absent category is what may be defined as 'Technical', that is, resorting to writing when some technical issue emerged. The 'Referential' label incorporates a large number of cases embracing the need to provide information, sometimes in the form of hyperlinks or files, as mentioned in Section 2.3.1. Instead 'Secrecy', 'Intimacy' and 'Fun/Kidding' require more detailed analysis. In the VIDEO dataset, 'Secrecy' is the second most frequent reason, as users often switch to

Applied Linguistics

writing when another person comes into the room or is within earshot, as emerges from the following:

Excerpt 13: I use the chat when my roommate is home and I don't want her to hear what I'm saying.

Excerpt 14: When I have to log out as I don't want my parents know that I'm still on FaceTime, I write down a quick message, so they don't know.

In theory, the 'Secrecy' category might be thought to overlap with 'Intimacy', but one way to distinguish them is the presence of an intruder, or 'unratified' participant in Goffman's participatory framework (Goffman, 1981). More specifically, 'Secrecy'-activated mode-switching has been classified as such only when meeting two criteria: (1) it is only from speech to writing and never the other way around; (2) the two main (ratified) participants want to prevent other unratified participants from hearing what they are saying. When these conditions are not met, speakers typically resort to writing to build up their rapport, in which case mode-switching cannot be explained as a 'secret' strategy, but as an 'intimacy-building' resource.

The 'Intimacy' category always involves two people but is hard to demonstrate as the users are, obviously, looking for privacy in their conversations. As Figure 5 shows, one notable exception comes from the MoM dataset, where, as

	Time	Participant	Speech	Writing	Mode-switching	Code-switching	Gaze	Kinesic action	Proxemics patterns	Visual units
46	18:19 – 4s	Irene		povero	+	+	Looks at the screen and then looks down to the keyboard.	Waits for the participant to talk with her left hand touching her head. Writes on the keyboard.	Only head visible.	
47	18:23 – 5s	Fred	//zee//		–	–	Looks at the screen.	Reads what's written. Sad grimaces	Only head visible.	
48	18:28 – 5s	Irene		ill be there so soooooooon	–	+	Looks down at the keyboard.	Moves backwards, writes something.	Goes out of the camera for a second. Head with no hair visible.	
49	18:33 – 1s	Irene	//ehm.. did you like that?//		+	–	Looks at the screen.	Smiles and touches her hands.	Half head and both hands visible.	
50	18:33 – 1s	Fred		zee	+	–	Looks at the keyboard.	Writes something.	Only head and hair visible.	
51	18:34 – 5s	Fred	//zee//		+	–	Oblique gaze.	Still.	Only head and hair visible.	
52	18:39 – 2s	Fred		zooon	+		Oblique gaze.	Writes something.	Only head and hair visible.	
53	18:41 – 5s	Irene	//zoooon...zee//	zoon	+		Looks down and back to the screen.	Writes, laughs and moves to her right.	Head and part of the arms visible. Very dark.	
54	18:46 – 2s	Fred	//zee//		¡		Looks at the screen.	Smiles.	Only head visible.	

Figure 5 Part of Irene's transcription grid.

reported elsewhere (Sindoni, 2019), an Italian student, Irene, included a personal video call with her English boyfriend Fred, based in London. The clip submitted as an end-of-course assignment was complemented by another two tasks: her written analysis and her short transcription of a relevant segment. Interestingly, and in keeping with many other examples in the MoM and EU-MaDE4LL datasets, she inserted a column to describe code-switching, in analogy with mode-switching, that signals the alternation between Italian and English, even though this column was not part of the pre-filled transcription grid provided to the students. Her code-switching category is discussed in greater detail in Section 3, as a translanguaging practice. Of the seventy-one transcribed turns (approximately 4':07"), a total of eleven code-switching moves,[7] and seven mode-switching moves, were transcribed by Irene, making this interaction rather rich for the purposes of this analysis.

An intimate situation is displayed both verbally and visually in this example as mode-switching reveals no explicit secret or excessively personal content. While Fred is more explicit in expressing his struggles of coping with a long-distance relationship, Irene seems to be more embarrassed and thus resorts to the written channel when Fred openly talks about him missing her. She turns to Italian and self-initiates mode-switching from speech, writing 'povero' (turn 46), meaning 'poor thing' in an affectionate way. As Fred replies saying 'zee', probably a way of imitating the Italian affirmative particle 'yes', Irene sticks to the written channel and replies with 'I'll be there so soooooooon', emphasizing with the number of 'o's in 'soon' the elongated sound and suggesting her anxiety to be there with him. After a further question from Irene, this time spoken, it is Fred's turn to self-initiate mode-switching, writing 'zee' and 'zoon', perhaps to mock the Italian voiceless alveolar sibilant /s/. Their creative and personal use of sounds is most likely a sign of intimacy that the written channel facilitates, as is recognized by Irene in her written assignment:

Excerpt 15: In turn 47, 50, 51, till turn 54, they both use the words 'zee' and 'zoon' that do not belong to any language and just represents their *particular use of language.*

Irene interprets mode-switching in the following terms:

Excerpt 16: Mode-switching is less frequent than code-switching and the participants only change mode at the end of the conversation. Irene

---

[7] I use the definition of code-switching throughout the Element only when specifically labelled as such by students. I prefer the term 'translingual practice' as it reflects my own theoretical approach, but I follow student's own definitions when they appear in their transcription grids and/or written analysis.

mode-switches in turn 46 at her own initiative, she starts writing and code-switches at the same time, because she writes something in Italian. The other participant continues in spoken mode and eventually mode-switches in turn 50 and 51 where he writes and speaks at the same time. Irene does exactly the same in turn 53 where she uses two modes to say the same thing. *This means that they are not mode-switching for a specific reason, such as bad connection, or because there are other people in the room, but simply to bring the other participant's attention to the screen and to their conversation by making them read instead of only listening.* However, by analysing the entire conversation it is clear that both participants' <u>preferred mode of communication is speaking</u> and that *they only write to catch the other's attention* (emphases mine).

Evidently, Irene recognizes the difference between 'specific reasons' (i.e., technical reasons) and other mode-switching functions 'to bring the other participant's attention to the screen'. While Irene does not explain this any further, this example shows how mode-switching can be used to increase intimacy and for building rapport rather than communicating referential content, such as questions or expressing agreement, for example with the use of emojis discussed above. Another American informant from the VIDEO dataset, Gloria, engaged in a long-distance relationship with Japanese Haru, confirmed the following:

Excerpt 17: Sometimes I felt awkward when it came to saying what I really felt. So I wrote down something nice, it feels less committing, you know what I mean? And especially when we were in the early stages of our relationship. I can't tell you why, but we used a lot of text chat.

In the interview, Gloria recalled her struggle to manage a long-distance relationship with a person from a different cultural context, mentioning several times that writing 'personal stuff' in the written chat alleviated her stress. As the relationship progressed and they got more used to each other's communicative styles, they started talking more openly using the spoken channel, but after two years, Gloria claims she still uses the written channel when she has trouble with expressing her feelings more straightforwardly.

A different form of mode-switching is displayed in the following example from the MoM dataset. Consistent with what was discussed in Section 2.3.1, the written channel is used here for reasons other than referential content and can be loosely grouped in the category of 'Fun/Kidding'. An Italian-American student, Ray, is talking to his Canadian cousin, Amanda, about her parents' refusal to

Turn	Participant	Speech	Writing	M	S	Kinesics	Gaze	Visual units
1	Ray					Ray grins, Amanda Is silent, nods and with a tight, forced smile	Ray looks upwards, Amanda looks sideways	
2	Amanda	[hesitant] Yeah.. but.. it's not/possible.. Because/number one/ I have no money because of university/				Ray raises his eyebrows	Amanda looks upwards while speaking Grins Smiles,	
3	Ray	yeah					nods	
4	Amanda	And number two/ he's still finishing and we don' know/ So/we're waitin'						
		ABRIDGED						
5	Ray	But your.. but what your mom said about this..? she/she..						
6	Amanda	No!						
7	Ray	No?						
8	Amanda	No! N-O Like this With a period!	No.	+			Mimics writing	
9	Ray	But why? Because she wants that you/ that you will marry before?						
10	Amanda	Yes.. she's very old school// No, she's very I-						
11	Ray	Italian						
12	Amanda	Yeah. Very Italian old school And what about						
13	Ray	your father? Like her.. no?						
14	Amanda	He's the worst. No. No. No like this So there you go.	No.!	+			Starts typing	

Figure 6 Author's simplified transcription of VMI between Ray and Amanda.

allow her to move in with her boyfriend before marriage. The exchange is reproduced in Figure 6 from my own abridged transcription. An inline video of the overall interaction is available by clicking the link in the Video 1 caption.

In this exchange, Amanda creatively employs mode-switching to add extra communicative power to her arguments. She talks about her parents' different

Video 1 Full interaction between Ray and Amanda. Video file available at www
.cambridge.org/Sindoni

reactions to cohabitation before marriage; hence she self-initiates mode-switching by writing down her mother's 'No.', adding 'with a period' (Turn 8) to signal
the definitiveness of her mother's position. As Ray giggles and enquires about
Amanda's father, she again mode-switches and writes 'No.!' with a period
followed by an exclamation mark, making it clear that her father's reaction was
'the worst' (Turn 14). In this case, punctuation allows her to complement her
spoken turns (6, 8, 10, 12, 14) with extra meanings. Interestingly, VMI further
contributes to the hybridization between speech and writing as stereotypical
language modes (see Section 2.1). Gestures can reproduce punctuation, such as
air quotes to signal that what is being discussed should not be taken at face value
(Cirillo, 2019), or air brackets to indicate that what is being said is incidental. In
this example, the conventions of writing are used within spoken exchanges, but
are reintegrated into writing. In other words, what were originally speech-specific
features (e.g., prosodic patterns, such as intonation) have been 'resemiotized' into
written typographic devices (e.g., punctuation meant to replicate prosodic patterns). Li and Zhu (2019) have discussed the practice of what they label as
tranßcripting, which is a form of writing, designing and playfully generating
new scripts by means of graphical and typographical devices by Chinese users in
digitally mediated social interactions. Even though this example could not be
described as *tranßcripting*, as it does not display excessively extreme forms of
script manipulation, it does nonetheless follow the same direction. VMIs allow a
further stage in resemiotization, that is, another semiotic transformation, as
Amanda's 'No.' or 'No.!' chat box input is part of spoken interaction that uses
writing to reinforce the spoken meaning. Writing in the chat box allows the
boundaries of the two language modes to be pushed to the limit, illustrating
how new and creative ways of making meanings are being developed by users.

3 Translanguaging Practices as Meaning-Making Resources

Translanguaging is a term that has gained increased currency in the last decade as it reflects the profound interconnections between cultures, peoples and societies and how these emerge in linguistic practices in creative and critical ways. The initial meaning of translanguaging, as coined by Williams (1994) and referring to the practice of alternating English and Welsh in class activities, comes close to the practice of language alternations examined in this Element, along the speech/writing continuum and across different languages. The alternation of language modes integrates with the use of different languages and varieties in VMIs, thus calling for explorations that account for these interwoven forms of language use. In this light, translanguaging practices are investigated in their alignment or disalignment with speech and writing in VMIs.

Broadly speaking, the core research into translanguaging is devoted to the study of learning pedagogies and language teaching in the context of bilingual and multilingual education. Theories about translanguaging have, however, evolved considerably over the last twenty years. Williams (1994) used the term to refer to the systematic use of two languages in classrooms, whereas Baker introduced the concept of translanguaging as a way for students to understand others and make meanings across different linguistic repertoires (Baker, 2011). A major epistemological shift differentiates code-switching from translanguaging: the former derives from a monoglossic view of bilingualism, which postulates that bilingual speakers 'possess' two distinct language systems, as if they were 'two monolingualisms', as aptly defined by García and Lim (2016: 119). The latter is instead characterized by a more dynamic view of 'languaging', where the integration of the various linguistic repertoires cannot be simplistically described as 'switches' from one language or one variety to another one, in a 'on/off' mode, but as a more complex and finely interwoven orchestration.

As already discussed in Section 1.2, Li has contributed to the theoretical development of translanguaging by designing the notion of *translanguaging space* that derives from sources other than those already discussed (Li, 2011). He locates his theory of translanguaging within the psycholinguistic notion of *languaging*, which refers to the process of using language to gain knowledge, to make sense, to articulate one's thought and to communicate about using language. Within this approach, languaging refers to 'an assemblage of diverse material, biological, semiotic and cognitive properties and capacities which languaging agents orchestrate in real-time and across a diversity of timescales' (Thibault, 2017: 82). It is a metareflective process, as well as an empowering practice that has profound ideological implications, pioneered by scholars working at the nexus between multilingualism, translanguaging and language ideologies that market language hierarchies, that is, Global North versus Global South (see, e.g., Bojsen et al., 2023; Mora, Tian & Harman, 2022a).

This position is consistent with sociosemiotic theories for meaning making and indicates lines of interpretation that go well beyond bilingual education. As Li clarified in an interview with Lawrence Zhang, translanguaging theories have in fact been applied beyond educational scenarios, including 'community sports, community business, community legal practices and community arts and heritage' (Zhang, 2022: 4).

The (multi)linguistic and multisemiotic repertoires of speakers will be observed in this section to investigate how they are strategically mobilized in video-mediated environments, so as to unveil their modes, media and language ideologies (Busch, 2018; Gershon, 2010a, 2010b). In Ho and Li's terms (2019), translanguaging involves the mobilization of learners' (and thus speakers') multilinguistic and multisemiotic resources. Consistent with this view, examples of multilingual video-based conversations will not be analysed simply in terms of 'speech' and 'writing' but will instead illustrate how the combination of differently named languages or varieties within the same conversation participate in the overall meaning-making process.

Translanguaging will thus be understood as a set of strategic and ongoing negotiations of one's own 'embodied repertoires' across and within languages and semiotic resources, such as those described by Zhu and colleagues (2020) in their specific contextual, sociolinguistic, translingual and cultural factors.

3.1 Translanguaging in Action

The *superdiverse* and *fluid* nature of languages in context has been increasingly reflected in research in recent years (Blommaert, 2010; Pennycook & Otsuji, 2015). Variation takes several semiotic forms in computer-mediated environments that involve heteroglossia and translanguaging practices (Androutsopoulos, 2011). As argued by Mora and colleagues (2022b), the combination of frameworks from translanguaging and multimodality is not new. Several studies have recognized the common identification of resources and modalities to make meanings, thereby acknowledging that speakers draw on a wide repertoire of resources that go beyond one language and one single modality for communication.

A notion common to both theories is that of *semiotic choice*, deriving from Halliday's model of social semiotics (1978). In order to make meanings, speakers make choices and do so by designing and constructing communication in different configurations that respond to their communicative needs and social expectations. Li directly refers to the tradition of multimodal social semiotics as shaped by the work of Gunther Kress (among others). Crucially, Li describes this integration as forms of resemiotization across diverse signs (2018: 22, my emphases):

> Translanguaging embraces the multimodal social semiotic view that *linguistic signs are part of a wider repertoire of modal resources* that sign makers have at their disposal and that carry particular socio-historical and political associations. It foregrounds the *different ways language users employ, create, and interpret different kinds of signs* to communicate across contexts and participants and perform their different subjectivities. In particular, Translanguaging highlights the ways in which *language users make use of the tensions and conflicts among different signs*, because of the socio-historical associations the signs carry with them, in a cycle of resemiotization.

Translanguaging is implemented within this ongoing cycle of resemiotization (Iedema, 2003). The arguments put forward by Li index three aspects motivating the integration of translanguaging with multimodality which help gain knowledge of what language users do to communicate. According to Li, (1) linguistic signs are only one part of the repertoire of the semiotic resources that speakers have at their disposal. This means that language is not given priority over other resources and modalities. (2) Language users can adopt different strategic configurations of resources to make meanings: how these will be combined is a matter of choice, but is influenced by socio-historical contingencies, habits and conventions. And (3) this process is not linear and straightforward: it implies a tension between what is conventional and what is disruptive and, hence, is quite often creative. In a similar vein, Lin (2015, 2018) speaks of 'trans-semiotizing' practices, where languages and varieties cross and are crossed by other semiotic modalities and resources. The following research questions will be addressed in the following sections:

- RQ1: How are interlaced multilinguistic repertoires represented multimodally by participants in transcription, annotation tasks and interviews?
- RQ2: How do language users make sense of their translanguaging practices in their VMIs?

3.2 Translanguaging in VMI

Translanguaging has been observed in VMIs in institutional and informal teaching and learning settings. Within the former, negotiation of meaning has been explored in tandem virtual exchange classes in Spain and Canada among Spanish-speaking and English-speaking students (Canals, 2021) and in the role of translanguaging to get feedback (Canals, 2022). Other studies have investigated online classes by video recording the embodied interactions using screen recording and multiple cameras as part of efforts to rethink static notions of language as an 'a-historical entity' and instead to navigate the ecosocial systems of learning across different timescales (Chen & Lin, 2022). Ho and Feng (2022) combine a translanguaging and multimodal model to scrutinize how an online English teaching video makes use of several semiotic resources, including translingual practices.

Studies have also examined multilingual identities beyond the classroom. For example, Schreiber (2015) discusses how a hip-hop artist mixes and mashes his Serbian and English identities in video communication in local and global communities. Adopting the perspective of digitally mediated communication and digital translanguaging space, Clabby (2021) analyses how individuals build their digital personas on an instant messaging platform. Other studies map evidence of learning based on comments on YouTube videos (Benson, 2015), as well as the impact of online learning and peer interaction after the Covid-19 pandemic, considering how students harnessed their resources to improve intercultural communication and how they recognized the empowering value of translocal identities (Ou, Gu & Lee, 2022). In the latter study, developing translocal identities can be achieved by giving pedagogical value to translanguaging practices.

An important focus that some research directions are taking is the recognition that learning is a transformative practice. These directions have been advocated by the reformist agendas in education discussed in Section 1. These can be pursued by means of alternative forms of learning, not necessarily confined to institutional contexts and traditional curriculum design. In this sense, Tai and Li (2021) highlight the role played by translanguaging as a pedagogical practice to motivate learners to exploit the full range of their multilinguistic and multimodal resources. To do so, they analyse the role of playful talk in an EMI (English Medium Instruction) mathematics class in Hong Kong (Tai & Li, 2021).

In the next section, some examples from the datasets used in this Element are discussed to see how individuals make sense of translingual practices as a metareflective process that mobilizes their cognitive, social and interpersonal skills, as evidenced in transcription tasks and interviews.

3.3 Translanguaging in Many-to-Many or Multiuser Interactions

As anticipated in Section 2.3.1, translanguaging practices are extremely common in platforms for instant video communication, where users come from diverse cultural and linguistic backgrounds. The 'Main Camfrog room', the first and only clickable one, is constantly populated with multiple language conversations, thanks to its permanently activated channels of communication, that is,

Figure 7 An example of translanguaging practices on multiuser video platforms.

the speaking floor and the chat box for written comments. These produce multiple overlapping conversations, rich in multimodal elements, such as distinct colours, fonts, emojis, GIFs and other multimodal 'gifts' that users can send to each other, increasing their status within the platform while at the same time receiving help themselves.

In the short extract reproduced in Figure 7, the languages used (in the order in which they appear) are Thai, English, Tagalog, Uzbek and Gujarati. The conversation, however, is hard to comprehend, as turns are clearly not sequential. A host of multiple micro-conversations co-occur, both in the spoken channel (Turkish and English when the screenshot in Figure 7 was taken) and in the written channel. A guide to follow the flow of conversation is the name of the speaker, who addresses one or more people using their mutual language of understanding.

Figure 8 illustrates a similar translingual situation and shows the alternation of Tagalog, Turkish and English. This second case illustrates how users expand the nature and extent of their dialogues by switching from one language to another and mode-switching from the spoken to the written channel. English generally appears to be preferred as the most 'open' and most intelligible language, whereas translingual practices are most frequently observed in the switch from one's 'first' language to English. The network of addressees, in this scenario, may be expanded or restricted according to language choice, as exemplified in Excerpts 18 and 19:

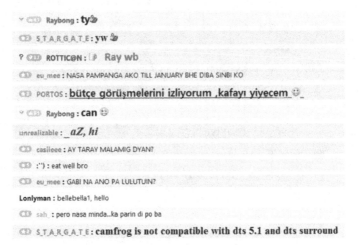

Figure 8 An example of translanguaging practices on multiuser video platforms.

Excerpt 18: I use Tagalog when I talk directly to my close friends. I use English when I talk to everyone in the room. Or I mix the two, or add another one, to get people confused, hahaha. How mean of me!

Excerpt 19: I am proficient in several languages as I've been a sailor for more than 10 years. That was so much fun, to learn languages, at least some bits and pieces. Now I can't travel as you know . . ., so I like to play with the languages I've learned and I keep learning from them. Yes, it's good to have all mixed up together. Languages are like a bunch of good friends to me!

Figure 9 quantifies the different types of reasons given for the use of translanguaging practices in the interviews, while Table 3 briefly characterizes the explanations given.

Even though some major differences between Table 2 (on reasons for mode-switching) and Table 3 are to be noted, some striking similarities emerge. Percentages of reasons in replies cannot be compared, as, between the first and second interviewee cohorts, the figures involved vary greatly, quite apart from their sociodemographic background, which could not always be collected or organized systematically.

The reasons for mode-switching (Table 2) show some correspondence with those provided by multiparty video platform users (Table 3). The most salient is VMI participants' willingness to fully exploit the playfulness and humorous potentialities of variation. The 'Fun/Kidding' category in the mode-switching domain mainly regarded the use of the written chat to increase the expressive power of their messages. This means that the written chat was used to add

Table 3 Reasons for translingual practices as provided by users (2020–22).

Secrecy	Wants to communicate content to one specific participant or a small group in the general chat and does not want to be understood by others.
Personal	Communicates personal content to one person who speaks the same language, using private chat (DM).
Fun/Kidding	Uses different languages for playful or humorous in-group jokes.
Local information	Provides background information in a language other than the one generally or specifically used at a certain point in a conversation.
Don't know	Not well aware about when and why they change language in interaction.

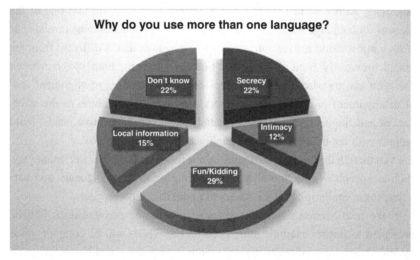

Figure 9 Percentage of reasons for translanguaging provided by users (2020–22).

humorous visual or other multimodal content, or to add jokes, commenting or overlapping with the main spoken floor of interaction. This use may be compared to what has been defined by Li and Zhu as Tranßcripting (Li & Zhu, 2019). The same category in the translanguaging domain plays a similar function: changing language or variety within the same communicative event is perceived to be 'fun' and therefore *strategic* when building a positively engaging digital persona. The 'Secrecy' category is likewise partially overlapping, as mode-switchers used the video affordances of writing content that had to be kept hidden from overhearers or 'unratified participants', to draw on Goffman's participatory framework (Goffman, 1981). In an equivalent manner, individuals who mixed languages during their VMIs claimed that this behaviour may be due to the need to restrict the wider number of potential addressees to a single individual or a small group in the multiuser room. Seen in this light, using a different language or variety marks in-group from out-group conversational dynamics. The 'Personal' category refers to one-to-one communication (most likely by means of direct messaging) and differs from the 'Intimacy' reason that mode-switchers resorted to when intense or intimate conversational moments arose. However, both the 'Personal' and the 'Intimacy' explanations indicate the intention, on the part of users, to build rapport within the Available Designs and within the modalities afforded by the medium.

The 'Referential' reason differs slightly in the two discourse practices, but is nonetheless comparable. Mode-switchers mostly claim that they use the written chat to give the discourse partners specific information, such as website addresses, names or to upload a file. Camfrog users explain that one of the reasons for language mixing is when local information needs to be provided or if such information is available only in one language that is different from the others previously used. Within the 'Secrecy' domain, both spoken/written variation and translanguaging practices serve the purposes of alignment and/ or disalignment in conversations. Users imaginatively combine media affordances and linguistic repertoires to satisfy their communicative needs, build rapport with the other users and discipline conversational chaos.

Even though the reasons and explanations for these forms of alternation vary, such as speech/writing and alternation/mixing of several languages and varieties, some similarities can be observed in the users' perceptions.

In the next section, some examples of one-to-one conversations will be presented to further examine other occurrences. These will be complemented by adding a sample of users' own perceptions and sense making in tune with multimodal and translanguaging theories of semiosis that highlight the agency and interest of the sign makers.

3.4 Translanguaging in One-to-One Interactions

The datasets used in this section have already been presented in Section 2.3.2. Hence all case studies introduced here draw on them for the sake of consistency. Returning to one example discussed in Section 2.3.2 and partially reproduced in Figure 5, Irene understood her and her boyfriend's translingual practices as 'code-switching'. It needs to be noted at this stage that not all students partici-pating in the project (and who had chosen video chat as the preferred digital text for analysis as their final assignment) had had formal instruction in sociolinguistics. They had diverse backgrounds and only a few small groups had studied general linguistics. None of them were familiar with theories of translanguaging. Furthermore, the transcription grid with the relevant categories of analysis did not feature either 'code-switching' or 'translanguaging practices'.[8] However, the students were invited to edit the transcription grid if they felt that some categories needed to be added or if others were not relevant in their video clip and could be merged or deleted. As a result, students from both the MoM and the EU-MaDE4LL projects had a certain degree of freedom as regards adapting the transcription table to their video materials and indeed proceeded to do so.

Since all video chats were in English, but with at least one participant speaking English as an additional language, some 70 per cent of all the video data included in MoM and EU-MaDE4LL datasets presents examples of translanguaging practices. A large number of students decided to add the category labelled as 'code-switching' in the transcription grid to represent the occurrence in question. This modification of the original transcription grid reveals students' language ideologies (see Li & Zhu, 2013), as they showed that they understood translingual practices as meaning-making systems worthy of separate discussion. When reading their written analyses, the reason they gave to explain these practices emerges as being mostly attributed to facilitating communication, as illustrated in the following example:

Excerpt 20: It's possible to see some spontaneous code-switching in French for Barbara, from minute 05:09 to 05:29, and in Italian for Tiziano, minute 5:20. The use of code-switching helps the two participants to explain the meaning of a word. Other examples of it are in turn 29 and turn 31, when Barbara uses the same technique to better explain what kind of object she is describing. In turn 14 at minute 01:08 Tiziano uses the word 'Duomo', that isn't a proper code-switching but a particular Italian word to indicate a cathedral.

In this example, Tiziano, an Italian postgraduate political sciences student, motivates his use of code-switching as a way 'to explain the meaning of a word'. Code-switching is defined as a 'technique'. It is unclear why he defines 'Duomo' as one 'particular Italian word'; it is probably because he considers 'Duomo' as untranslatable and therefore such a term cannot be explained in terms of code-switching

---

[8] The categories of analysis included in the grid were: (1) time; (2) participant; (3) speech; (4) writing; (5) mode-switching; (6) gaze; (7) kinesic action; (8) proxemic patterns; (9) visual units (screenshot). However, students were allowed (and encouraged) to edit the transcription grid if they thought that the video clip they had to analyse presented other relevant categories and/or if they wanted to edit, merge or cut some categories.

or as a form of translanguaging. Other students with a background in linguistics show a much more refined ability in unpacking the interactional functions of translanguaging, even when the latter is not explicitly identified.

Excerpt 21: The chosen clip of the interaction between S and T is an interaction in which S is teaching T Italian phrases. Mode-switching (MS) is an essential resource used in this section of interaction as it enables S to visually display the Italian phrases and T to grasp a greater meaning of what S is teaching her. S uses the *Skype* messaging system to type what she has previously said . . . . This allows for S to convey technical information which may be construed if only delivered orally. The use of MS also allows for T to reinforce her knowledge and facilitate learning the new language. There is a common pattern that emerges when MS is employed in this section. S types the word, T pronounces it and then S repeats and/or corrects what T has just said.

In this scenario described between S (the secondary participant) and T (the author of the excerpt, an English 'native' speaker), use of mode-switching once again runs parallel to the combined use of two languages (in this case, Italian and English). The written channel is used for informal teaching purposes and T, the English speaker, implicitly recognizes that changing languages is part of the communicative repertoire that usefully facilitates intercultural communication. Even when using this basic and improvised teaching strategy, T mobilizes all the resources at her disposal, such as 'superior language knowledge' and media affordances to facilitate communication. Translanguaging and mode-switching are equally identified as viable solutions that improve intercultural communication, as made explicit in the following (my emphases):

Excerpt 22: S tended to use more mode-switching to *facilitate intercultural communication* when the words she needed to communicate were in Italian. . . . T's attempts at reading the word aloud and S's follow up demonstrate that both participants are invested in the conversation. Displaying their shared engagement indicates their genuine interest in their discourse partner, *enabling intercultural communication*.

As Excerpt 22 shows, the use of the written and oral channel is interlaced with translanguaging practices and is not directly addressed in the discussion. The video interaction displays that mode-switching is finely interlaced with translingual practices. The learner's comments are also indicative of her perception of symbolic power coming from her position of 'native speaker' (see Zhu & Kramsch, 2016). Her commitment to facilitating interaction resonates with the argument made by Zhu: 'conversation involvement refers to the psychological solidarity and connectedness individuals show to each other through active participation in interaction' (Zhu, 2019: 106). Figure 10 shows a portion of the transcription grid produced by Veronica in conversation with her German friend Barbara.

In this example, the column labelled 'Code-switching' is inserted by Veronica to show the change from English to German as taking place in her interaction with her German friend. However, no mention of this event is made in her written assignment. The positioning of the column alongside the column on 'Mode-switching' reveals how the two forms of language alternation can work in partnership in VMIs. The conversation is about Christmas presents. Veronica is the first to start using German in this conversation section, by saying 'Weihnachtsmärkte!' (a turn not reproduced in Figure 10). Then Barbara repeats 'Weihnachtsmärkte! Ya, jawohl!', thus confirming in her language the typical folkloristic venue evoked by her friend. She confirms that these places are similar everywhere as they imitate the German Christmas markets and then writes down the city in question, that is, Leipzig. Veronica initially confirms the name, but then she corrects her friend and tells her the exact place she had in mind in the first place, that is, Stuttgart. What is to be noted here is not so much the change in language (as naming cities in their original language is not a noteworthy translanguaging practice in itself), but how Veronica makes sense of the overall exchange. Unlike Tiziano, Veronica considers naming German cities as 'code-switching' and, as such, feels the need to update the transcription table. This means that she values these examples as language changes, from English to German, even though she does not elaborate on these occurrences in her written assignment and only says:

Excerpt 23: At the minute 14:34,22 mode-switching was accompanied by code-switching: 'Leipzig'. Another moment of code-switching was at the minute 13:50,00: 'Weihnachtsmärkte!'.

In fact, the two occurrences of mode-switching are paired with two occurrences of the use of German. Whether interpreted as language change or as mere reproduction of the name of the two German cities, this is yet another example of how these practices are intermingled, and not by chance, with the creative use of the spoken and written channels in video chats.

Another example of translanguaging can be found in the case exemplified in Figure 11.

The whole interaction can be viewed by clicking the link to inline Video 2 in the footnote.

Time	Participant	Speech	Writing	Modeswitching	Codeswitching	Kinesic action	Gaze	Proxemics patterns	Screenshots
13:51,21	Barbara	Weihnachtsmarkt ja, jawohl!		−	+	Touches her glasses with her right hand	Oblique gaze	Very close shot, light setting, two objects visible (the curtain and the kitchen cupboard)	
13:54,29	Barbara	It looks like in Germany actually, because it was a German city before, before the war		−	−	Places her face on her hand	Oblique gaze	Very close shot, light setting, two objects visible (the curtain and the kitchen cupboard)	
14:34,22	Barbara		Leipzig	+	+	writes	Looks at the keyboard	Very close shot, light setting, two objects visible (the curtain and the kitchen cupboard)	
14:41,22	Veronica	Ah Leipzig! No!		+	+	reads	Looks down in order to read	Both settings within the screen	
15:03,29	Veronica	Stuttgart!		−	+	Moves her finger, gesticulating	Oblique gaze	Very close shot, light setting, three objects visible (the door and two photos)	

Figure 10 Transcription grid as modified by Veronica.

Row	Time	Participant	Speech	Writing	Mode-switching	Code-switching	Proxemics patterns	Kinesic action	Gaze	Setting (built environment)	Visual units (screenshots)
1.	00:01	T	// I-I-I don't remember if/ when I did the.. uhm.. the [interview...] /	–	–	–	Positioned at the left side of the screen	Moves his hand close to the screen then lowers it	Looks up to his right, then gives a brief look at the screen then turns to his left	Sitting with his back to a window from which comes a bright light. Close to the screen, full head and a bit of his shoulders visible	
2.	00:06	M	// [Yeah] //	–	–	–	Positioned at the centre of the screen	Slightly tilts her head and nods	Looks at the screen	Sitting in a blue room with her back to a door from which comes a bright light. Head and shoulders fully visible	
3.	00:06	T	//'cause I'm not gonna do interviews/ I-I get nervous.. [I remember] /	–	–	–		Shakes his head	Looks at the screen		
4.	00:10	M	/[Mpf I know!] //	–	–	–	Moves slightly away from the screen then back closer	Laughs			

Figure 11 Transcription of interaction between Mariangela and Tonino (part 1).

Video 2 Full interaction between Mariangela and Tonino. Video file available at www.cambridge.org/Sindoni

This transcription grid comes from the EU-MaDE4LL dataset. The interaction is between a student participating in the project and her Canadian-Italian cousin Tonino. As a Canadian-Italian, Tonino quite often switches from Canadian English to Italian, as he knows Mariangela will understand him effortlessly. More importantly, these translanguaging strategies increase solidarity between participants. The conversation is about the different degrees of confidence in face-to-face versus video-recorded interviews. Both discourse partners recognize that being recorded adds a sense of awkward self-awareness that impinges on overall performance. As shown in Figure 11, Mariangela identifies what she labels as 'code-switching' as a significant resource in video interaction and, as such, adds a column to transcribe all its occurrences. Later on in the interaction, Tonino laces his Italian with the use of a typical idiomatic expression, that is, 'al volo', which means 'without prior notice, quickly, without preparation'. This short exchange is reproduced in Figure 12.

In this second part of the transcription in Figure 12, Mariangela reports on the comment made by Tonino, who was forced to give an interview 'al volo', therefore switching to Italian and taking advantage of the expressive power of this Italian idiom. 'Al volo' captures the improvised nature of the social request imposed on Tonino and his unwillingness to comply with it. This language choice is taken up in Mariangela's written assignments. She explains this choice in the following terms:

Excerpt 24: Another interesting factor happens around 01:40 (row 25) when he switches from English into Italian for a specific expression, that is 'al volo', an all Italian practice in his opinion, that he feels he can exactly express only using a different language.

Row	Time	Participant	Speech	Writing	Mode-switching	Code-switching	Proxemics patterns	Kinesic action	Gaze	Setting (built environment)	Visual units (screenshots)
24.	01:16	Mariangela	// I talk a lot but.. In front of the camera it's.. different //	–	–	–		Laughs a bit then shrugs and raises her hand to drop it immediately after	Looks at her right then back at the screen		
25.	01:22	Tonino	// So I.. I don't remember if now in the interview that's going on tomorrow if I spoke about.. If I	–	–	+		Moves a bit going back to a previous topic, trying to remember	Looks up and around pensively then looks at the screen		
			mentioned that uhm you guys are doing something with Iva Zanicchi or not / I don't remember.. It's 'cause these guys don't get you prepared and I'm like "Send me quest" / he told me that "No andiamo al volo" / Yeah / andiamo al volo... //					then laughs at his own words while moving his hands around to indicate the Italian expression and fidgeting			
26.	01:42	Mariangela	// Mmhh yeah //	–	–	–		Smiles	Looks at the screen		
27.	01:43	Tonino	// Everything Italian is / everything is al volo and I'm [like] /	–	–	+		Keeps smiling while moving his hands	Looks at the screen		
28.	01:45	Mariangela	// [Yeah!] //	–	–	–		Smiles and nods while shrugging	Looks at the screen		
29.	01:46	Tonino	// "Thank you" //	–	–	–		Smiles jokingly	Looks at the screen		
30.	01:48	Mariangela	// That's true //	–	–	–	Turns on her seat before going back to the previous position	Laughs	Looks at the screen then bottom right then back at the screen		

Figure 12 Transcription of interaction between Mariangela and Tonino (part 2).

In this example, language choice functions to express the exact feeling that Tonino wishes to convey, and Mariangela captures his translanguaging practice to increase his rapport with her, as she shares the same language knowledge. An analogous situation can be observed in another VMI from the EU-MaDE4LL dataset. The Italian student Francesca is interacting with her British friend Jake. Drawing on her basic knowledge of linguistics, Francesca equates all translanguaging practices as 'code-switching' and makes sense of these practices as follows:

Excerpt 25: The shift from one language to another one is known as code-switching, that describes any switch among languages in the course of an interaction whether at the level of words, sentences or chunks of language. Heller (1988) approaches code-switching as a form of verbal strategy, which represents the ways in which the linguistic resources available vary and the ways in which individuals draw on the verbal resources to achieve shared understanding. Referring to the video chat, code-switching occurs in different occasions, at minute 00:07, 00:13,21, 00:13,25 and 00:13,27. It is other-initiated code-switching.

In her attempt to be scientific in her assignment, she unproblematically defines any form of language mixing as 'code-switching', drawing on classic literature in the field of sociolinguistics and refers to variation. She then makes it clear that the use of more than one language has to do with how speakers draw on their linguistic repertoires to achieve communicative goals, which could be building rapport or mutual intelligibility. These functions of language change are explored in Excerpt 26:

Excerpt 26: At the beginning Jake greets me saying 'ciao' immediately signalling 'sympathy' between us and later he uses the word 'teatro' while he was trying to remember something he saw when he was in Italy.

In the first reported example, 'ciao' is the almost universally acknowledged Italian informal greeting, which Jake uses to signal 'sympathy' in Francesca's words, by recalling his past experience of being an Erasmus student in Italy. He then uses the word 'teatro' when attempting to recall another past experience, namely visiting the ancient Greek theatre in Taormina with her. Figure 13 shows how the exchange is reproduced in the transcription grid filled in by Francesca.

Jake here brings into play his linguistic repertoire (and reminisces on his basic knowledge of the Italian language) to recall past memories that he shares with Francesca. The latter, as other students had done in both the MoM and EU-MaDE4LL datasets, makes sense of the interaction by adding another column in the transcription grid, labelled as 'code-switching', perhaps in analogy with the 'mode-switching' column. In this case, even though all the communication is brought forward in English, fragments in Italian contribute to building common ground for intercultural communication.

These examples of translanguaging arise and are made sense of outside the classroom context. This means that they are not pedagogical or designed by a teacher; they were neither used as specific class strategies by the researchers participating in the project, nor explicitly taught in the syllabus. They were defined and described by students as 'code-switching', in keeping with a classic and popular definition readily available to university students with no background in sociolinguistics, and even less knowledge of translanguaging theories. However, these examples have been presented and discussed in this section to show how translanguaging practices emerge spontaneously when people from distinct cultural and linguistic contexts interact and are also recognized as meaning-making 'resources', as explicitly defined by the student Francesca.

Role	Time	Participant	Speech	Writing	Mode-switching	Code-switching	Proxemics patterns	Kinesic action	Gaze	Setting (built environment)	Visual units (screenshots)
3	00:13,17	Jake	//[A theater] or something like?/		–	–	Close shot, positioned at the centre of the screen, head and shoulders visible	Sitting, moves the right hand, smiling, right hand put in his right temple	Looks at the screen	Sitting with a blue wall, a mirror and a rack of clothes on his back	
4	00:13,18	Francesca	//It was a thea .. a .. uhm/a greek theater//		–	–	Close shot, positioned at the centre of the screen, head and half upper body visible	Sitting, moves right and left hands, gesticulating, touches her hair, small head movements and then nodding	Direct gaze, looks at the webcam then oblique gaze and back to direct gaze	Sitting with a white wall and paintings on her back	
5	00:13,21	Jake	//Yeah yeah /wat's that - what's that in italian tea-teatro [or]?/		–	+	Close shot, positioned at the centre of the screen, head and shoulders visible	Sitting, small head movements, nodding and smiling	Direct gaze, looks at the webcam then oblique gaze, and back to direct gaze	Sitting with a blue wall, a mirror and a rack of clothes on his back	

Figure 13 Francesca's transcription grid.

This section has made use of the same datasets but reflected on these practices *a posteriori*, as they spontaneously surfaced in VMIs and were not explicitly taught in class. This *a posteriori* analysis was not meant to explore language choices, but to primarily assess if, how and to what extent learners recognized and interpreted translingual practices. Occurrences and frequencies, as well as the explicit mentions and explanations given by students, provide insights into how these are perceived and unpacked in terms of language ideologies, especially because students had received no overt teaching on these issues.

4 The Repurposing of Gaze in Video-Mediated Scenarios

In Isaac Asimov's novel *The Naked Sun* (1956), one of the characters claims that seeing interlocutors face to face and viewing them on screen is quite different. When challenged by another character, she replies that seeing is only possible face to face, because one can merely 'view' an image on screen in mediated contexts (quoted in Baron, 2000). Even though the difference may seem trivial, the implications between what is *seen* in person and what is *viewed* through mediational means, such as a computer or mobile device screen, needs to be addressed and understood by participants, both in educational and professional contexts.

Looking at other people, and being looked at in return, is an example of one meaning-making semiotic system in human interactions that works in partnership with language, but which is able to produce meanings *independently* of language or even *in contrast* with what is said verbally. In a face-to-face dialogue, for example, conversation may well include turns that are realized only with gaze, for example to indicate a wide and varied range of communicative epistemic and evaluative functions and emotions, such as dis/agreement, solidarity, surprise, shock, uncertainty, and so on. These silent turns can usually be understood by the other with no effort and with no need to use language to explain what is being conveyed by gaze. Additionally, these gaze-based meaning-making turns can *contradict* what is said, for example when a person says 'Sure!' while rolling her eyes. Verbal and visual meanings work together and there is no way to establish which of the two meanings guides or prevails over the other.

However, most language-based perspectives consider gaze as language dependent, as may be inferred from labels defining it as 'paralinguistic' or 'non-linguistic', and implicitly suggesting that gaze makes meanings that are necessarily secondary or dependent on language (see, e.g., the foundational study by Sacks, Schegloff & Jefferson, 1974). For example, gaze has been analysed as a conversation 'facilitator' in CA, such as to signal transition relevance places (TRPs), that is, when one can give or take the floor of conversation (Goodwin, 1980, 1989; Kendon, 1967, 1990b). In the domain of social psychology, Kendon highlighted the expressive and monitoring functions of gaze, as well as its role in regulating the flow of conversation by turn-taking. In his research, he noted that individuals looked at their partners for about 50 per cent of the time, looking more while listening rather than while speaking. When speakers start an utterance, they tend to look away, but at the end of the turn, they focus their attention on their partners (Kendon, 1990a, 1990b).

Eye contact is likewise highly dependent on context and plays several roles, such as information seeking, signalling interpersonal attitudes, and controlling the synchronizing of speech and prosody through gaze shifts. Mutual gaze can build intimacy, while the lack of it allows avoidance of undue intimacy. Inhibited gaze dodges excess input of information through distraction (Argyle et al., 1973; Argyle, 1976; Argyle, Furnham, & Graham, 1981). In interactional sociolinguistics, it has also been shown that when speakers do not find a looking listener, they either produce syntactic breaks and hesitations, or stop the conversation until gaze comes back at them. Thus, while breaks request the listener's eye contact, pauses are used to stimulate the interlocutor's gaze (Goodwin, 1980).

Particularly in one-to-one interactions, gaze plays a fundamental role in displaying visual engagement, signalling alignment or disalignment with the other discourse partners, shaping actions and regulating the flow of conversation (Rossano, 2012, 2013). Some studies have argued that gaze is not organized in turns-at-talk in ways similar to those of speech, even though gaze follows the organization of speech (Heath, Hindmarsh & Luff, 2010). Gaze in fact accompanies speech in regulating the transition from one speaker to the next in the process of turn-taking (Goodwin, 1979, 1980). Multimodal approaches to interaction have shown that gaze may work in combination with speech but within the orchestration of 'multimodal ensembles' (Geenen & Pirini, 2021), in which no mode is given prominence a priori.

Eye contact and gaze exchange are specific features in face-to-face conversations that vary across cultures but are generally organized by speakers to successfully manage turn-taking. However, media affordances in VMIs have radically changed the picture in terms of gaze behaviour (Bohannon et al., 2013; Monk & Gale, 2002). The achievement of perfect eye-to-webcam alignment is by no means a reality on most digital platforms, even though systems of gaze correction have been developed and further refined in the last few years. Intel developed a model for eye-contact correction in video chats using deep neural systems (Fadelli, 2019) and, more recently, the proof-of-concept research prototype, FutureGazer, has been designed to leverage Processing IDE,

JavaScript and Unity Game engines to build an eye-and-head model within a simulated web video conference environment (He, Xiong & Xia, 2021). However, webcams are still typically placed on top of video devices, thus making eye-to-eye alignment troublesome. They have been so since the beginnings of VMI (Vertegaal & Ding, 2002), a trend which seems to be here to stay.

As a crucial communicative resource, gaze has been the focus of research in face-to-face instructional contexts, for example as co-occurring communicative gaze for information-giving purposes (McIntyre, Mainhard & Klassen, 2017), as well as in video-mediated educational settings, for example as a source conveying the speaker's attitudinal stance (Crawford Camiciottoli, 2021). Other studies have explored gaze management in VMI, such as organizational strategies within frameworks of social presence (Satar, 2013), space management in sign language instructional contexts (Hjulstad, 2016) and visual access to learning materials in telepresence classrooms (Jakonen & Jauni, 2021). On the whole, educational research in language learning contexts has placed emphasis on measurable task performances, such as to what extent gaze behaviour regulates or influences a given outcome, such as in task completion, understanding, turn-taking management, and so on.

Ever since the Covid-19 pandemic started tearing through many of the world's countries, video apps, such as Apple FaceTime, Microsoft Teams and Google Meet, have foregrounded questions about gaze management in video-mediated personal, educational and business interactions (Tschaepe, 2020). Recent studies have tackled the 'repurposing' of gaze, for example finding that English learners' meaningful looking at their peers' on-screen image correlates with successful meaning negotiation in synchronous VMIs (Li, 2022). Combined approaches, such as CA and interactional linguistics, produce multimodal and sequential analyses of 'simultaneous start-ups', when two participants' initial turns overlap in the video-mediated tutoring of English as an additional language (Malabarba, Oliveira Mendes & de Souza, 2022). Other research has shown how gaze, in partnership with other resources, can encourage or daunt learners' 'willingness to communicate' (WTC) in multimodal settings (Peng, 2019). Problems with eye contact, or unsuccessful eye contact, are particularly disruptive when people do not share the same context. These disruptions go beyond turn-taking management and may lead to conversational breakdowns.

The mismatch in eye contact or 'forced skewed visuality' (as defined by Kaiser, Henry & Eyjólfsdóttir, 2022) may lead to misinterpretation and discomfort, creating a sense of confusion and frustration among learners. Even though research is making great strides in addressing these issues, broader questions of gaze management, organization, patterning and interpretation in VMIs may benefit from sociosemiotic and multimodal perspectives. These transcend the technical constraints and look at how lack of mutual gaze and other aspects of gaze impact on how meanings are interpreted (Sindoni, 2019).

One of the medium-specific affordances of gaze in VMI is that reciprocating gaze is much more troublesome than in real-life contexts (Friesen, 2014; Sindoni, 2014). In other words, a participant either looks at the webcam, hence projecting the feeling of 'being looked at' to the other discourse partner, or directly looks at the screen, so seeing the other – but not looking them straight in the eye (Sindoni, 2011). Within these digital scenarios, participants either *look at the webcam* and therefore simulate eye contact for the other, or *look at the screen*, thus seeing the other but, at the same time, failing to simulate eye contact.

Problematic distributions of gaze in video-conferencing environments have been and continue to be addressed in computer science (He, Xiong & Xia, 2021), but the consequences for the semiosis of interaction still need to be fully mapped and discussed (Hietanen, Peltola & Hietanen, 2020), especially when it comes to educational environments (Satar, 2013). For example, as a side effect of webcam positioning and a platform's in-built affordances, users may visualize their own projected image while speaking, thereby activating a set of constant self-monitoring strategies that alter acceptable time lags between conversational turns (Sindoni, 2019). Other research has shown that change of settings and background in video-based mobile calls shapes interaction (Licoppe & Morel, 2014). From an educational standpoint, the 'obtrusiveness' of gaze (e.g., a *surveillance gaze*, as defined by Jones, 2020) in remote teaching and learning settings also needs to be considered relevant. These improvements of teachers' cultural awareness and media responsibility when 'viewing' students' personal spaces are fundamental to ensure safe and inclusive online classes.

The research questions dealt with in this section are:

• RQ1: How is gaze, as a conversational facilitator, refunctionalized and 'resemiotized' in video-conferencing platforms?
• RQ2: How do participants unpack and make sense of media-constrained affordances of gaze in mediated environments?

The following sub-sections investigate how media affordances shape gaze patterns and organization and how participants adapt to such affordances by 'resemiotizing' gaze (Iedema, 2003; Sindoni, unpublished data).

4.1 The Lack of Mutual Gaze in VMI

In keeping with the other sections of this Element, participants' understanding of how gaze is exchanged and distributed in VMI is foregrounded. Individuals, as sign makers, make sense of gaze patterns and comment on the various implications that media affordances have on their interactions and on the meanings exchanged.

One example from the MoM dataset helps gain some insight into learners' meaning making vis-à-vis gaze behaviour. Figure 14 shows a screenshot of a Sri Lankan travel agent who lived in London at the time when the video call was recorded.

Linda is captured in this and other screenshots in very close-ups and her gaze behaviour is described in the following terms by her discourse partner Zoara (my emphases):

Excerpt 27: Linda always has a direct look at the screen. She hardly seems to look at her own image in the small close-up frame, and when she does it her look is very quick and almost indiscernible: just a glance. But, a salient element we do not have to forget is the fact that *she is using a smartphone: Skype images and frames are considerably smaller on a Skype app than they might appear on a laptop or pc screen.* This aspect might be misleading when analysing gaze, since *its directionality is not clear cut.* Nonetheless, whenever Linda is talking, *she mostly moves her eyes away from the screen,* while she tends to *turn them back in a more direct position as soon as she wants to underline a word, or she has decided her speaking turn is over or she is asking a question to her partner.*

Zoara demonstrates a remarkable level of awareness about gaze behaviour and discusses several aspects of it at some length. First, she mentions that Linda is

Figure 14 Linda looking at the screen.

using a smartphone for her video call, thus significantly reducing the size of her image. Zoara realizes that this medium-afforded reduction in visibility may well influence her interpretation of gaze. She points out that gaze directionality can sometimes be hard to detect in VMI. She then describes how Linda manages gaze. In her interpretation, when Linda speaks, she tends to avoid direct gaze, whereas she does the opposite when specific moments arise in the interaction, such as when she wants to 'underline a word' (i.e., emphasis), has 'decided her speaking turn is over' (i.e., signalling turn completion) or is 'asking a question' (i.e., requesting the other to take the floor). All these gaze patterns can be interpreted as accompanying speech in keeping with CA approaches that conceptualize gaze as an important visual cue (or 'visual method', as described by Ford & Thompson, 1996). However, Zoara goes beyond this and continues her explanation as follows (my emphases):

Excerpt 28: *Her gaze is never reciprocal* and she never looks straight to the camera *with the intention of giving the impression of looking at her interlocutor in the eye.* From *a psychological point of view* we might say the fact she *mostly moves her eyes away from her partner's ones (actually from the screen)* is a symptom of *shyness, embarrassment and even of a little bit of insecurity.*

What she expresses in Excerpt 28 shows that Zoara comprehends media affordances regarding the problems in reciprocating gaze. She raises the question of *intentionality*, as she takes for granted that looking at the webcam serves the purpose of 'giving the impression' of reciprocating the gaze of the other. Looking straight at the webcam entails a degree of unnatural gaze patterning in that this visual behaviour forces the participant to divert their eyes from centre-screen, where the items discussed in the interaction are displayed. A high degree of awareness is needed to change this behaviour so that the other discourse partner 'feels' a more natural interactional situation. In other words, conveying a sense of natural gaze use implies forcing oneself to look at the webcam instead of looking at the other discourse partner's projected image (Sindoni, 2013). Quite strikingly, Zoara interprets this state of affairs as a 'psychological' personality trait rather than attributing such gaze behaviour to inadequate media affordances (i.e., webcam–eye disalignment). Her 'psychological' interpretation is, however, moderated by other contextual factors that in her view may well affect the screen-mediated conversation, as reported in Excerpt 29:

Excerpt 29: But we also have to remember this is not a face-to-face conversation, so, the fact itself that the two participants are not sharing the same context, they are located in two different countries, with a considerable time-zone lag, might negatively influence the level of interpretation of the meaning-making resources.

Here, Zoara hedges her 'psychological' interpretation of Linda's gaze management by listing some contextual factors that may impact on communication, such as different physical locations where they are placed and the considerable time lag involved, as Zoara is temporarily living in Australia. She is able to explore all these various components by mentioning features that are not exclusively linked to turn-taking management, but which surpass the verbal. These suggest that the 'interpretation of meaning-making resources', as she puts it, is much more complex and involves resources that transcend language-only data.

The VIDEO dataset reveals that the difficulties of conveying a sense of natural gaze behaviour was acutely felt by some other participants. An American teacher of English in one high school based in Brazil, Thomas, submitted clips of his online classes after the Covid-19 pandemic for my research project. Screen captures cannot be reproduced here to protect his students' anonymity, but we viewed the clips together and discussed at length the problems he had regarding the offline/online transition. In one of the post-recording interviews, which took place in May 2020, I asked him what the main challenges he was facing were. Excerpt 30 reproduces part of his answer:[9]

Excerpt 30: Students were not always compliant and did not turn the webcam on. I usually do a lot of eye contact in my classes to check understanding and see that they're following me. On Zoom I was completely lost. I was teaching in the dark, d'you know what I mean? When I had some grammar to explain, like some rules, I wanted to have them follow me and tried looking at the cam quite consistently. To have them feel I was talking to them, to get their attention. But, you know what?, it was hard, it all felt so unnatural and fake to me. I didn't keep my eyes on the cam as much as I thought. And my eyes seem erratic, oh my!

Thomas was intensely self-conscious of his gaze behaviour, because his face-to-face teaching methods relied heavily on eye contact to check his students' understanding. He had been teaching in Brazil for more than twenty years, so his cultural knowledge of the context, his students' class behaviour and their expectations were high. However, the pandemic turned all his past experiences upside down. He tried to reproduce his usual gaze behaviour in video environments and reported that he had realized from the very beginning that he needed

---

[9] Excerpt 30 has not been reproduced verbatim, as we had four interviews in total and the transcriptions are extremely long and some concepts are repeated in similar forms and phrasings several times.

to look at the webcam to convey the feeling of 'being looked at' to his students, as a technique to maintain their attention and exercise a form of control. However, he recognized that it had been difficult to keep this up consistently and that such contrived gaze organization (i.e., forcing himself to look regularly into the webcam) led to inconsistencies and 'erratic' eye movements.

The VIDEO dataset includes several other participants who reported similar circumstances. When the video conversation took place in personal settings and for mundane activities, efforts that failed to achieve perfect mutual gaze were not perceived as a problem and 'adaptation to the medium came out naturally' (as one VIDEO informant put it). Conversely, lack of eye contact and/or eye–webcam misalignment surfaced as one of the major causes of breakdown in communication when checks were made to establish whether communication had been successful.

Another example from the EU-MaDE4LL dataset points to different facets of this visual event being interlaced with mode-switching. A Danish student involved in the project, Freja, set up an experiment with her long-time friend Mariana, a Portuguese girl living and studying zoology at the University of Nottingham in the UK. While Mariana knew in advance that she would be recorded for some project by Freja, she was not aware of the details of the research project. The Facebook video call was therefore quite natural (at least for Mariana) and presented an intimate conversation between the two close friends. However, Freja was quite surprised that Mariana had agreed to being recorded in a restaurant, with considerable background noise and distraction. Freja had decided to see her friend's reaction to a (fake) revelation over the video chat to see if and how Mariana would react, given the social constraints of being in a public space. In normal and relaxed conversation, Freja had recognized Mariana's attempts at eye contact as being very low, somehow hinting at little involvement and null emotional investment in the conversation, but things changed abruptly as Freja announced that she was going to make a shocking revelation:[10]

Excerpt 31: Suspense was heightened as she stared into the screen while nodding to signify that I got her full attention. This point was especially important as it introduced the mode-switch and thus change in context. While I moved the image of [VISUAL IMAGE EXPLAINING THE REVELATION] to the messenger window, she put a finger at her mouth corner and moved in towards the screen, as if she was expecting a big surprise (Still 8). Interestingly,

---

[10] The content of this fake revelation is not reported here. Even though both participants signed the consent form, this revelation (albeit fake) presents sensitive content and is not relevant to the topics discussed here.

Figure 15 Still 8 from Freja's transcription.

after she received the picture through messenger, she had to look down at her phone (Still 13) in order to see it (channel-switch). But from Still 8 until Still 16, there is not a single moment of her gaze wandering off horizontally but instead only vertically. This suggests that the noise distractions from her setting seemed irrelevant once I created this urgent, suspenseful matter of revealing the [CONTENT OF REVELATION].

To provide more visual context, the stills mentioned by Freja are reported in Figures 15 (Still 8) and 16 (Still 13).

As documented in Excerpt 31, Freja was building up suspense, and so Mariana adjusted herself to receiving the news, both in body movements, moving closer to the camera, and by showing with a highly focused gaze direction that Freja had all her attention. However, instead of revealing the content of her announcement with words, Freja decided to send Mariana a picture via the Facebook chat. The mode-switching from speech to visual content initiated by Freja was followed up by 'channel-switching' (as effect-ively described by Freja herself). This refers to Mariana's change of device, switching from her laptop, used for the conversation, to her mobile phone, to see the image revealing this surprising content. This channel change, from laptop to mobile screen, most likely due to the pressing need to get immediate access to the visual content sent by file, was defined by Freja as 'channel-switching' in the written assignment, once again detailing the participants' critical and creative skills in construing the meaning making of VMIs

While Figure 15 reproduces Mariana's slight change in attitude, less formal and slightly closer to the screen, anticipating Freja's revelation, Figure 16 neatly

Figure 16 Still 13 from Freja's transcription showing Mariana's genuine surprise.

shows Mariana's genuine reaction of great surprise that needs no verbal content to be understood, either by Freja herself during the interaction, or by future viewers of the screenshot. Mariana's bewilderment is conveyed exclusively by means of gaze, which, regardless of the screen constraints discussed in this and the previous section, visibly reproduces what could have happened in a face-to-face context.

This example is telling as regards both Mariana's reaction conveyed through gaze alone and despite the media-dependent problems of gaze management in VMI, and Freja's overall meaning making. In her analysis, Freja in fact commented on Mariana's extremely restrained reaction when compared with the shocking nature of the revelation. She had expected a more dramatic reaction, such as raising her voice or jumping up from the table. This is particularly true as Mariana came 'from a very temperamental and exotic culture, Portugal', but 'it came across that she tried to adapt to the common rules of British society in a public place'. Interestingly, Freja manifested her cultural assumptions and stereotypes about Mariana by taking for granted that because she comes from an 'exotic' culture her reaction would be far more dramatic. In the case study here illustrated, Freja makes cultural assumptions based on Mariana's country of origin, Portugal. Considering it to be a 'very temperamental and exotic culture', Freja expected a different reaction. Mariana's reaction, interestingly, is not projected exclusively and strictly in linguistic terms, but is framed in broader terms, including observations of her socially inscribed movements, body positioning and eye behaviour. In this sense, Freja's written analysis helps unearth students' expectations, cultural biases and hypotheses that surpass the mere organization of gaze patterns in VMIs. This form of understanding can be gained by means of a combined multimodal and translanguaging approach that aims to unveil semiotic, plurilinguistic and cultural ideologies. More specifically, drawing attention to all multimodal non-verbal resources that contribute to meaning making can help students, or any other participant interested in improving communication skills in video-mediated environments, to reflect on the many facets that determine whether, and to what extent, communication is successful. Even though learning and teaching are largely based on language-based contents, these case studies show that multimodal communication, if properly scrutinized, can produce insights on how meanings are assumed, produced, circulated and understood in different cultural contexts. Cultural assumptions, in this specific case, seem to rest more on generalized ideas of what one essentialized culture may be in the eyes of the observer (in this case, Freja's) more than on specific individual personality traits and behaviour (in this case, Mariana's).

These observations should guide further reflections on how meaning making transcends not only linguistic and cultural boundaries, but even individual and personal ways of understanding and perceiving other people's knowledge making.

4.2 Self-Looking and Gaze Sequences

Since the very beginnings of my research into VMI, the media affordance of self-looking has emerged as making video interaction quite different from face-to-face situations (Sindoni, 2011, 2013, etc.). I defined this media affordance as if we were constantly looking at a mirror placed within close sight while having a face-to-face conversation. This self-conscious feeling would, I predicted, be greater than normal and would cause several self-monitoring adjustments (Sindoni, 2013).

The infographics reproduced in Figures 17 and 18 partially report results from interviews I conducted with separate batches of participants in 2011–13 and 2020–22, respectively. They draw on data already reported in Figures 2 and 3, but focus only on the practice of self-looking. Even though, as mentioned in Section 2, the results are not comparable for several reasons, mostly because the participants were different and because the number of interviewees varied greatly, what remains constant is the high percentage of participants claiming that they look at themselves during a video chat, that is, 74 per cent in the first batch and 92 per cent in the second batch (but with 75 per cent fewer participants).

In the more detailed interviews conducted in 2020–22, all participants claimed that their answer referred to informal, personal, mundane situations in one-to-

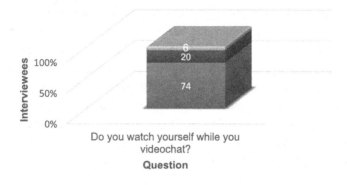

Figure 17 Self-looking by interviews (years 2011–13).

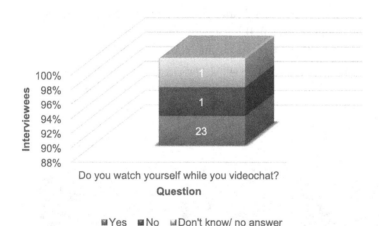

Figure 18 Self-looking by interviews (years 2020–22).

one contexts that always called for leaving the webcam on. 'No-one would dream of switching the webcam off' in one-to-one contexts, as one informant explained. Having the webcam on implies the extremely likely action of self-looking during video calls.

On the contrary, gaze directionality in multiparty video interactions is harder to discern; even though we may infer a certain amount of self-looking, this is unlikely to be visually perceived by others in interactions. Furthermore, building on the consideration reported above on the unlikeliness of turning the cam off in one-to-one scenarios, it can be assumed that this improbability tends to decrease in multiparty environments, as the social pressure to be 'visible' is weaker. In post Covid-19 educational scenarios, the question about how much the request to turn on the webcam during classes imposed on learners has been discussed at length elsewhere (Sindoni, unpublished data). What can be deduced from digital field observations is that in multiparty scenarios, gaze directionality – and related questions of self-looking – remain unclear even when all cameras are turned on. This can be seen in Figure 19 (with users cartoonized using the Picsart Editor app to protect anonymity) following the vectoriality indicated with arrows.

In some of the interviews reported above for the second batch, the participants clearly distinguished their gaze behaviour in terms of self-looking by reflecting on the diversity of one-to-one versus multiparty interactions, specifying that when they had the chance to switch off the webcam, the possibility of self-looking automatically dropped out, sometimes to their great relief.

Some deeper insights into learners' reflections on self-looking can be found in the MoM and EU-MaDE4LL datasets. Yet another example of how learners made sense of this medium-specific affordance comes from Zoara, who explains and interprets the meaning making of this feature, even though she defines this behaviour in 'psychological terms', by discussing the possible reasons for self-looking:

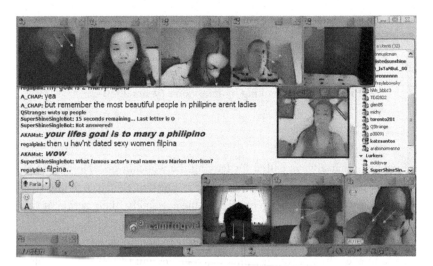

Figure 19 Complex gaze directionality in multiparty video platforms signalled by arrows.

Excerpt 32: The main reason could be a *narcissistic* one: people are clearly influenced by the vision of their own image, thus trying to adjust it to their own best expectations. In other words, to look better. It is self-evident that this impending presence on the screen also affects the naturalness of the interaction, apart from increasing the sense of detachment due to the lack of reciprocity in gaze.

Zoara interprets self-looking as a signal of narcissism, making it clear that it means appearing at one's own best. Self-monitoring, however, can influence the naturalness and spontaneous quality of one-to-one conversations, as Zoara points out, connecting this last point to the general sense of detachment produced by the lack, or limited amount, of meaningful eye contact. Another student from the EU-MaDE4LL dataset describes this event in the following terms (my emphasis):

Excerpt 33: During the videochat, direction of gaze was mainly oriented towards the other participant in both cases, which creates an impression of the individual gazing centrally at the screen or slightly downward depending on the position of the webcam. However, an interesting sequence which occurred on several occasions throughout the interaction was a series of *'self-checking'* *gazes*, where the individual looked at the projection of their own image before reverting to the centre of the screen.

While the student described how participants in the conversation managed gaze directionality by gazing centrally or downward the screen, she also identified some sequences defined as 'self-checking gazes'. To illustrate these sequences visually, the student inserted the screenshot with arrows reproduced, unedited, in Figure 20.

Another example from the MoM dataset is meant to illustrate how self-looking is finely ingrained in gaze sequences. Figure 21 shows a gaze sequence portraying Barbara, a translator from Luxemburg.

Section A on the left-hand side portrays the beginning of the conversation. Barbara gazes at herself, looking right downwards at her close-up frame. In Section B, Barbara matches her gaze direction with what she is saying: 'It's a wonderful day here!', thus directing her gaze out of the window. In Section C of Figure 21, she looks downwards, as she is silent and listening to (and therefore looking at) her interlocutor. This gaze sequence further illustrates how self-looking and gaze vectoriality and directions are finely interlaced and can be understood in context; only in some cases were the participants explicity asked to recall what was going on at that specific moment in the interaction.

Screenshot showing the notion of self-directed gaze

Figure 20 Example of self-looking as described by one student (i.e., self-directed gaze).

Figure 21 Gaze sequence.

In what follows, movement organization and distribution space will be investigated, as well as the reframing, or resemiotization, of social distance in VMI.

5 The On-Screen Distribution of Movement and the Construction of Distance

This section will discuss examples of how embodied interaction is instantiated and repurposed in video-based platforms, with reference to interlaced forms of mediated embodiment, such as kinesics and proxemics. The former refers to how movements are indexically organized in typical patterns of meaning making (Harrigan, 2005; Martinec, 2004) and the latter (Hall, 1966) deals with how social distance is projected onto the screen in socially motivated configurations of meaning making that contribute to the orchestration of embodied repertoires in multilingual and multicultural settings (Zhu, Li & Jankowicz-Pytel, 2020).

In VMIs, physicality and corporeality are dematerialized (Paech, 2012) and usually only a portion of the person is captured on screen (e.g., head and shoulders, with occasional framing of torso). Video conversations occur in simulated *in praesentia* contexts, where embodiment concurs with other resources and modes. Screen-mediated bodily presence adds new meanings in multilingual and multicultural scenarios, for example in terms of how the interpretations of movements vary across cultures and in terms of how webcam positioning produces framing of participants (Licoppe & Morel, 2014; Sindoni, 2013). Webcam positioning determines how close or distant each individual is captured on screen, thus projecting social distance according to a webcam's position and not reflecting how physical bodies are arranged in situated real-life contexts.

Research has shown that kinesic and proxemic patterns influence the way in which the online *persona* is presented in digital environments, for example as 'intrusive' or 'inquisitive', if the webcam positioning projects the participant in an excessively close shot (Sindoni, 2014). Hence a lack of awareness about these dynamics may cause possible misunderstandings and even disrupt the communicative flow. As research has shown (Heath & Luff, 1992; Sindoni, 2013), the messages that imply, or can be interpreted as, social imposition may arise from mere technological setup (e.g., with regard to webcam positioning) or by the physical placement of members on screen (e.g., by being more or less proximal to the screen). Even though these messages may be unwanted, they are tolerated to a lower or higher degree according to experience with the medium, styles, preferences and culture. If some mis/use of on-screen movements and distance may be considered acceptable in some social, linguistic or cultural contexts, poor or improper handling of these may have a negative impact on communication in other situations and/or cultures. The absence of intercultural knowledge may lead to communication breakdown.

The research questions addressed in this section are:

- RQ1: How can intercultural communication be improved by increasing awareness about the forms of embodied interaction?
- RQ2: What are the different affordances and constraints of video-based client platforms and how can these be used to facilitate video interactions?

5.1 Kinesic Patterns, or How Body Movements Shape VMIs

The study of kinesics, or of how movements contribute to shaping communica-tion, is linked to language-based theories of communication. Kinesics was named as such by Birdwhistell (1952) and developed out of the general research area of non-verbal communication. Kendon likewise mapped the domain by identifying movements in all their visible and communicative functions (Kendon, 1990b, 1997, 2004).

The 'non-verbal communication' label itself reveals questions of language dependencies and forms of hierarchies, as the negative prefix 'non' seems to implicitly point to a 'secondary' nature of gestures and to derivative, language-dependent ways of organizing space in communication. Halliday, for example, recognizes that gestures play a regulatory function in cooperation with language: 'to control the behaviour of others, to manipulate the persons in the environment' (Halliday, 1973: 31), while the psychologist Goldin-Meadow (1999: 428, my emphasis) argues that 'gesture provides speakers with another representational format *in addition to speech*, one that can reduce cognitive effort and serve as a tool for thinking. Gesture also provides listeners with a second representational format, one that allows access to the speaker's unspoken thoughts and thus *enriches communication*'. The underlying assumption here is that, yet again, movements are considered derivative and language dependent, as a corollary to the main meaning making provided by language.

Social sciences have developed several models to study and categorize gestures, for example, within domains such as psychology (Goldin-Meadow, 1999; McNeill, 2005), anthropology (Haviland, 2004; Kendon, 2004) and language-based disciplines, such as CA (Goodwin, 1979; Schegloff, 1984; Streeck, Goodwin & LeBaron, 2011).

Multimodal studies consider movements in their contribution to meaning making in partnership with or independently from language, according to the situation and people involved. For example, Kress and colleagues (2001) have given a detailed account of the fundamental role of gestures in classroom contexts. More recently, multimodal research has significantly advanced knowledge of how movements cooperate with other multimodal resources, such as facial expressions, gaze, posture, social distance, head movements and manipulations of physical objects and surroundings in embodied interactions (Mondada, 2016; Mondada & Oloff, 2011). Lim (2021) makes a strong case for the pedagogical relevance of the use of gestures in classroom practice and develops a systemic functional approach to increase teachers' awareness of the pedagogical effectiveness of gestures in combination with language and other resources. In VMIs, Norris (2004) mapped the study of gestures and movements in spatially constrained environments mediated by the screen, by categorizing movements along the *continuum* from full intentionality to unintentionality. As the definition of *continuum* suggests, it is not always possible to distinguish between intentional and unintentional movements, especially in in-between situations. If pointing is certainly intentional and posturally preferred positions are surely automatically triggered behaviour, other halfway body movements are not so clear-cut. For example, it would be hard to find agreement about whether the hand position of a MoM participant reproduced in Figure 22 is

Figure 22 Hand position: intentional, half-intentional or unintentional?

intentional, half-intentional or unintentional. However, in this specific context, we focus on how meanings are made and received.

Hand gestures, body movements and body positioning have been variously classified. Some distinguish between communicative functions of hand gestures, such as *deictic* (e.g., pointing and context dependent), *motor* (e.g., batons and beats, facilitating rhythm and pace), *symbolic* (e.g., emblems, conventionalized), *iconic* (e.g., visual representations of a referential meaning) and *metaphoric* (e.g., visual representation of an abstraction, see McNeill, 1992).

As key components in human communication, movements, gestures, positioning and facial expressions all contribute to meaning making in interactions. However, VMIs pose a further challenge to their interpretation. As argued in more detail elsewhere (Sindoni, 2013, 2014), the medium-specific affordances of video platforms and apps in desktop or mobile devices only allow a small portion of the participants' bodies to be viewed. This is particularly true in the case of mobile communication, when only head movements and possibly occasional postural shifts can be captured by the other discourse partners on screen (Licoppe, 2009). Assuming that the webcam is on and other discourse partners can be seen, this body 'fragmentation', or partial reproduction of the whole bodily presence, needs to be taken into account when making meanings and interpreting other people's meaning making in interaction. Teachers, educators and practitioners in the field of language policies, syllabus planning and remote learning need to be aware of the diverse features facilitating or hindering smooth VMC.

In multiparty interactions from desktop devices, several single hand gestures and sequences can be found in Figure 23, which compiles twelve screen captures of users in different situations.

Some hand gestures in Figure 23 are *iconic* in that they are used to represent a concrete object visually and referentially (Stills 1, 2 and 9), size (Stills in Sequence 3 and 4) and quantities (Still 5 and Stills in

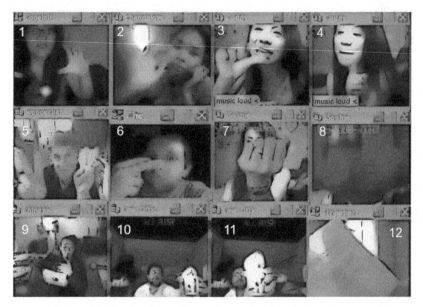

Figure 23 Hand gestures by multiparty video call participants.

Sequence 10–11). Other hand gestures are symbolic, such as the emblems in Still 2 (waving) and Still 6, which playfully mean 'I'm watching you'. Still 9 represents the deictic gesture of pointing, as does Still 12, where the user Strawberry is pointing at the screen with a sheet of paper. These screenshots are illustrative of several kinds of hand gestures that can reproduce the face-to-face context and even create a sense of proximity to the other speakers. Some gestures can be understood universally, such as waving or pointing, and their use can help build empathy in environments that are, by definition, fragmented and disconnected from each other.

One of the EU-MaDE4LL students highlighted that intercultural communication can be encouraged and facilitated by the use of gestures, revealing her language ideologies as an English 'native speaker' (see also Sweeney & Zhu, 2010):

Excerpt 34: Some interesting observations from the current videochat include smiling and nodding performed by the native speaker and specific hand movements made by the non-native speaker, as well as gestures with universal meaning used on both parts. From a semiotic perspective, common gestures such as waving and pointing are beneficial in intercultural communication because they can be interpreted by both sides.

Utterance and description of action	Screenshot of action
I'm sorry my *pronunciation* is not the best (left hand touches neck)	
uh and the exam was about philology so how Russia was born and all the *history* (rolling arm gesture)	

Figure 24 Kinesic action described by one EU-MaDE4LL learner.

In Excerpt 34, the learner feels the need to specify that smiling and nodding was performed by the English native speaker, whereas the non-native speaker (defined by status negation) uses 'specific hand movements'. These are further explored in the assignment, partially reproduced in Figure 24.

In the assignment, the learner explains that smiling and nodding are used as accommodation strategies (Sweeney & Zhu, 2010) to confirm comprehension and prompt the 'non-native speaker' to continue conversing. On the contrary, some hand gestures made by the non-native speaker are employed with the following functions:

Excerpt 35: Hand gestures 'act out' some of the references she makes throughout the conversation, which represents a form of clarification of the utterance and may be beneficial when issues with pronunciation occur in intercultural communication.

The learner conceptualizes two different 'sets' of facial expressions and gestures, assigned to native and non-native speakers on the grounds of diverse (symbolic power) positions in asymmetrical conversations (Zhu & Kramsch, 2016). Even though the native speaker is genuinely keen on engaging the non-native speaker in a smooth conversation by adopting several strategies to save the non-native learner's face, at the same time, she indirectly points to her own implicit (native) linguistic superiority.

Another instance from the same dataset provides an illustration of reversed roles: the non-native speaker, Sara, teaches some Italian words to the English native speaker. Motor gestures, batons and beats, are used to provide coherence by means of a finely interlaced combination of language, prosody, and rhythmic hand and head movements, as described by Matilda below:

Excerpt 36: Sara nods her head rhythmically whilst saying the phrase in a similar rhythm, this adds a musical quality to her utterance. This type of gesture opens Sara's body language and invites Matilda to repeat the Italian phrase after her. The musical quality adds an element of fun and encourages Matilda to speak in her non-native language.

In other cases, gestures serve to contextualize the environment and have a 'showing' function, what I have defined elsewhere as *displaying* hand gestures (Sindoni, 2018). Displaying hand gestures lead, partially or entirely, to substituting the projected image of the participant with an object or the visual availability of the immediate surroundings. Licoppe and Morel aptly defined the default configuration of VMIs as 'talking heads', where participants 'show as much of their face as possible' (Licoppe & Morel, 2014: 4). However, in the situation described in Excerpt 36, the consequences of movements and gestures are a momentarily entire or partial disappearance of the person described as the 'show-er' (contrasted with the 'viewer' in Licoppe & Morel, 2014). Some examples are shown in Figure 25.

The stills in Sequence 1 and 2 reproduce a user who is moving an empty bottle of wine close to the screen. This is a displaying gesture. Turning the bottle upside down is a gesture that is used to prove visually what he is saying verbally, that is, that the bottle is empty. In the stills in Sequence 3 and 4, another

Figure 25 Sequences of 'show-ers' in *displaying* mode.

participant is showing some banknotes he has just earned. Yet again, showing corresponds to adjusting distance between oneself and the object in question vis-à-vis the screen. In turn, these movements equate with providing evidence of what is being said. The noteworthy medium-specific affordance here consists in the entire (Still 2) or partial (Stills 1, 3 and 4), yet momentary, disappearance of the shower. In a face-to-face context, hand movements do not change or obscure the bodily presence of all the involved individuals, however extended these hand movements may be. This paradoxical VMI affordance has been noticed by learners, as can be seen in the following excerpt:

Excerpt 37: [The participant's image is in] a frame that hides some movements like, for example, keyboard typing or everything else that could possibly distract the participant while having the conversation. ... This displacement involves an obstructed visibility that hides completely or in part the participant.

These comments reveal the learner's awareness about the 'dual nature' of this medium-specific affordance. If, on the one hand, the partial (and screen-based) reflection of the other discourse partner helps diminish distraction (for example, when one of the two is typing, thereby detaching him/herself from the other's direct eye focus), on the other hand, this displacement results in a contrived sense of fragmentation, 'an obstructed visibility', as vividly put by the student. Another learner from the EU-MaDE4LL project worded the in/visibility question in the following terms:

Excerpt 38: The close-up shots of the participants limited how much of each participant was visible, therefore affecting what gestures and movements were visible. Overall, the participants used a combination of semiotic resources to construct an intercultural conversation and it appears that as the interaction progressed, Sara and Matilda became increasingly comfortable with each other.

In this passage, the learner quite nicely captures the possibilities and limits (or to use Kress' (2005) words, 'gains and losses') of gestures and movements in screen-constrained environments. Despite the unattainability of full access to the other discourse partner's bodily presence, adaptation to, and metapragmatic awareness of the medium, contribute to mutual intelligibility.

5.2 Proxemics, or Staged Social Distance in VMI

The cultural anthropologist Edward T. Hall coined the term 'proxemics', meaning 'the study of social distance', as 'the interrelated observations and theories of humans' use of space as a specialized elaboration of culture' (1966: 15). In broad terms, proxemics deals with how people put distance between

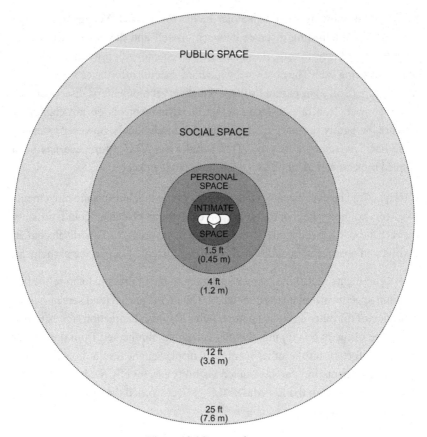

Figure 26 Personal space.

WebHamster, CC BY-SA 3.0, via Wikimedia Commons

themselves and others according to cultural, social and personal relations and conventions. Hall described personal space by clear-cut categories according to physical distancing. These are presented in Figure 26 in feet and with metric conversions.

Personal space deals with the areas very close to the individual, whereas territory refers to larger surroundings that are controlled by the individual, such as the office or a specific chair in a conference room to gain a sense of privacy. Invasion of personal space or violation of what is considered by the person to be a private territory may lead to serious discomfort and communication break-down. Goffman defines personal space as the 'space surrounding an individual, anywhere within which an *entering* other causes the individual to feel encroached upon, leading him to show displeasure and sometimes to withdraw' (1971: 29–30).

However, as can be detected from Figure 26, the concept of proxemics needs to be completely revisited in screen-constrained scenarios, as *all* forms of interactions, whether personal, professional or public, are structured as if they *were* taking place in intimate spaces. This medium-specific affordance was identified by Grayson and Coventry (1998) who discussed the effects of visual proxemics in VMC. More recent studies investigate how distance in mediatized communication needs to be reframed vis-à-vis media affordances (Drąg, 2020).

In earlier research (Sindoni, 2011, 2013, 2014), I contended that proximity or detachment is fixed and frozen in video calls, because distance is not established between people in interaction, but between one individual and one machine, be it a desktop or mobile device. All forms of culture-dependent and socially constrained measures of distance are reduced to *intimate*, as the usual arrangement of space is that of 'talking heads', as described by Licoppe and Morel (2014), with only heads and part of the torso visible. The distance between oneself and others in VMI is therefore not semiotically built and engaged with in social interaction, but rather *staged*, meaning that it is enacted through technical arrangements, dealing with the participants' positions in relation to the webcam, such as close, far, frontal, oblique or even absent if the webcam is switched off.

As discussed in Section 5.1, bodily presence and movements, as well as engagement with objects and physical surroundings, is constrained by screen framing. Furthermore, closeness or detachment are determined by webcam positioning that can be self-consciously adjusted by participants or, conversely, disregarded. Hundreds, if not thousands, of YouTube tutorials on video communication surfaced when the Covid-19 pandemic hit, and gave practical tips and suggestions on how to adjust webcam position, framing, lighting and setting to appear in the best possible light, or, to use Zoara's words from Excerpt 32, 'to look better'.

Users of multiparty platforms for everyday interactions do not seem to observe the 'social codes' of proxemics in VMI, producing feelings of awkwardness, as mentioned by some interviewees. The top 'discomforting' positioning was reportedly the oblique one. Similar reactions have been detected in the much smaller sample interviewed in 2020–22. Noticeably, no suggestions in my questions were made with reference to the kind of position that caused negative feelings. The extent of discomfort, combined with a negative evaluation of the other's digital literacies, is summarized in the following comment:

Excerpt 39: What annoys me most is when the other is not frontal. Like he is. [indicates an oblique line with hand and arm] . . . No, this is too disturbing, it's

Involvement ←→ detachment

Viewer power ←→ equality ←→ participant power

Figure 27 Subjective attitude in interactive visual meanings (adapted from Kress and van Leeuwen, 2020: 143).

... they don't give you attention, or are too dumb to know how to make video calls. No way I can get it!

In semiotic terms, this feeling of scarce attention or detachment articulated in various ways by the interviewees is consistent with theories of visual semiotics. An obvious source is the famous distinction between frontal angle as representing involvement and the oblique angle representing detachment made by Kress and van Leeuwen (2020), with reference to how interactive meanings are produced visually in terms of attitude. The attitude of the sign maker (i.e., the one who produces the visual sign) can be analysed as subjective and objective. Subjective attitude is summarized in Figure 27.

Even though Kress and van Leeuwen analysed forms of visual design and not of spontaneous face-to-face interaction or VMIs, their categorization applies to all datasets and research on VMI in this Element. Some example screenshots of oblique positioning cartoonized participants with the Picsart Editor app are shown in Figure 28. These are all taken from multiparty video calls.

As Figure 28 shows, oblique angles are extremely frequent positions in which users are (self-)framed. This is due to webcam positioning that takes the participant sideways, albeit with varying degrees of obliqueness. Despite the frequency of this *visual social framing*, users seem to agree on the sense of detachment that this configuration produces, most likely unwillingly, in all those that 'receive' (i.e., see) this image projection. However, all instances in Figure 28 reproduce the 'talking head' configuration and, as such, succeed in maintaining contact with the other viewers. When asked about this framing, one user from the Philippines pointed out that he had never paid attention to this feature and explained this behaviour as follows:

Excerpt 40: Never mind, no one is interested in it. You don't talk to a single friend, but to a bunch of people all at the same time, so no one sees where you are.

Jerry was certainly right when commenting on the diverse framing expectations in multiparty versus one-to-one conversations; however, most users (roughly 72 per cent) reported on a negative feeling if and when the other discourse partners

Figure 28 Multiparty video chat users in oblique angle.

had been viewed sideways, even though this framing did not generally lead to communication breakdown, but only a 'bad disposition' towards the others.

However, other webcam positionings seem to go even further, as shown in Figure 29.

In this case, bad lighting in Row A, Figure 29, limits what can be seen of the discourse partner. While excessive proximity disturbs viewing in Row B, undue distance as 'staged' in Row C equally troubles the discourse partners' viewing. All these forms of framing contribute to 'staging' participants in positions that do not facilitate communication, but rather create a sense of 'distance', 'awkwardness', 'weird positions' and 'detachment', as variously phrased by the participants. As these multiparty platforms for VMC are increasingly popular,

Figure 29 Staged distance in multiparty video calls.

improving awareness about the meaning making of multimodal resources for communication is essential in personal, professional and educational contexts.

As nicely put by one learner, proxemics should be understood as broader than the mere arrangement of webcam positioning in VMI and should incorporate other contextual features that may facilitate, or, quite the reverse, prevent smooth communication.

Excerpt 41: Studying all the different aspects treated by the various fields of studies, I think that what really makes the difference in video chats are the participants that are 'acting in' (taking into account their behaviour, manner and culture) and which kind of relationships is already (or intended to be) established between them. *Maybe these factors should be considered part of proxemics.* Which in video chats is described physically as *the distance between the participant and the media and what surrounds him/her.* But proxemics at the same time is *the social relationship among participants as well.* So, it is impossible to not consider at the same time: the strength of the intention of the participant and the setting of situation he is living in. That feeling is supported by the illusionary perception of contextual presence of video chats.

Both kinesics and proxemics are closely intertwined in VMIs and produce meanings that may vary across linguistic, social and cultural perceptions. Proximity and distance are made sense of in different ways in diverse contexts. What is shown, what is not shown, as well as how bodies, objects and surroundings impart meanings in screen-constrained environments, are other facets of video communication that alter what is generally possible (and impossible) in face-to-face interactions.

6 Conclusions

As shown with examples in this Element, awareness of the multiple differences between interactions in face-to-face versus mediated video contexts is crucial when facilitating communication in multicultural and multilingual scenarios. Emphasis has been placed not so much on measurable criteria related to the improvement of performance in a certain educational context (for example, in English-language learning and teaching settings), but rather on the process of sense making of several kinds of participants, including but not limited to learners from diverse social science backgrounds. Understanding and making sense of the 'Available Designs' in VMIs can be improved by increasing familiarity with the communicative epistemological differences that have a technological basis at the surface level (e.g., online communication by means of a screen but from diverse locations). At a deeper level, these differences *go far beyond technology* as they accelerate forms of distinct semiosis across communities, individuals, cultures and languages. These differences are instantiated in translanguaging spaces. The development of critical, multimodal, translingual and multicultural literacies is key in this process (Sindoni et al., 2019; Vasta & Baldry, 2020). This approach is meant to align with the proposal of a 'practical theory of language' advocated by Li (2019).

While synchronous video interactions *apparently* seem to reproduce real-life interactions, they afford new possibilities that include the alternation of written and oral channels of communication, as well as the chance to increase the degree and extent of translanguaging practices. The translingual repertoires of language users in VMIs can be variously deployed and harnessed for several communicative purposes, such as restricting and expanding the range of addressees – within time frames alternating in rapid succession and even with the overlapping of spoken, written and translingual turns.

The answers to the RQs in Section 2 are that participants do use *mode-switching*, that is, the medium-specific affordance of alternating speech and writing in VMIs, in a consistent way. This option is not impossible or excluded in face-to-face contexts, but is restricted to some situations and not normalized as much as it is in VMI. For various reasons discussed in Section 2, mode-switching has been defined as a medium-specific affordance, in that *the technological possibility has been turned into a semiotic recursive act.* The talking functions of switching from speech to writing in the text chat box in VMIs are varied and include broad categorizations such as 'Secrecy', 'Intimacy', 'Fun/Kidding' and 'Referential'. These categorizations are not clear-cut and are not intended as top-down or prescriptive rubrics. They may help increase metapragmatic awareness of media affordances and guide learning and teaching, as well as the development of successful communicative strategies in personal and professional settings.

Moreover, the use of the written text chat box is not restricted to language, but has come to include other multimodal materials, such as images, emojis, emoticons, GIFs, as well as hypertext materials that direct to other digitally mediated environments, such as links and documents. The written chat box is used creatively by users to add, mix, re-mesh and comment, as well as to gain an additional floor for conversation, especially when the spoken floor is already taken or when there are multiple competing and unmonitored open floors (mainly in multiparty video interactions).

When it comes to language use, however, multimodal resources are not limited to speech and writing. In this Element, I have argued that various languages and varieties used in communication make meanings in distinct ways, as they can signal affiliation and distance in multiparty environments, for example by restricting or expanding the selected addressees. In multilingual video platforms, where conversational chaos is very likely to occur, a core strategy to open, keep and select multiple floors is to change and/or mix languages and varieties for several communicative functions. These uses have been described and compared to the functions identified by the participants themselves for the mode-switching pattern. These functions include 'Secrecy', 'Personal' (slightly different from the 'Intimacy' function in the spoken/written alternation), 'Fun/Kidding' and 'Local information' (yet again dissimilar from the 'Referential' function in the spoken/written alternation).

Even though these categorizations have been identified and grouped *a posteriori* by the author of this Element and may reflect an interpretative bias, the reflections found in the written assignments on VMI produced by learners in two projects support this interpretation and provide insights into the learners' sense making of translingual practices. If mode-switching was an explicit category of analysis in the two educational projects,[11] translingual practices

---

[11] As found in the transcription grid and part of the taught content in the students' syllabus, both in the MoM and in the EU-MaDE4ll project.

and strategies were not part of the taught content in their syllabi and therefore were not targeted by the learners (or the teachers) in their written assignments about the multimodal analysis of their own video interactions. Notwithstanding this content gap, learners were ready to identify and describe translingual practices spotted in their interactions, even though they had not been asked to do so in their transcription and written assignments. They almost unanimously recognized these practices as 'code-switching', as they had no background knowledge in translanguaging theories. Despite incongruent labelling, their meaning making of these events has been investigated in this Element to document their sense making in both their transcription tables (with learners' additions of a further column, labelled 'code-switching' in analogy with 'mode-switching') and in their written assignments. Their observations lead to the consideration that developing metapragmatic awareness and metalinguistic reflection can be an autonomous and creative process for learners (Busch & Sindoni, 2019). In this respect, learners' language ideologies, their opinions and implicit beliefs on languages, can be deduced from transcription tasks and written assignments, as well as by general surveys and interviews, irrespective of the participants' background. All these thoughts are not explicit forms of learning, but represent invaluable material for promoting broader and more informal forms of learning, inspired by the reformist agendas concisely discussed in Section 1.

Multimodal communication plays a role in this overall process of semiosis in VMI. Gaze has been repurposed in screen-constrained environments, because media affordances have called for other forms of adaptation. Among the forms of repurposing of gaze that respond to the RQs addressed in Section 4, the lack or reduced degree of mutual gaze, as well as the affordance of self-looking, have been identified as crucial indicators of pragmatic disalignment from face-to-face encounters. The latter generally allow a close and spontaneous adaptation to other interlocutors' bodily presence, which includes a range of meaningful cooperative strategies, such as eye contact and mutual gaze accompanying speech, as well as head and hand movements that can parallel, complement, integrate and substantiate what is being said verbally. However, I have contended that what have been considered as 'language-derivative' or 'paralinguistic' systems of semiosis actually work in parallel with language. This means that these systems can be understood in isolation in several scenarios and, as such, are independent meaning-making systems of semiosis. In a similar light, kinesic and proxemic patterns in VMIs contribute to interaction in distinct ways, organizing communication, facilitating (or interrupting) turn-taking and, more broadly, conveying a sense of affiliation or detachment that can be analysed in orchestration with language choices. However, kinesics and proxemics can make meanings independently from language. The fact that all these systems *can work in isolation to produce meanings does not mean that they should be interpreted in isolation.* I argue for unpacking semiotic resources in communication along the lines indicated by Baldry and Thibault (2006) with the aim of exploring how they individually contribute to meaning making. This is a bottom-up approach that has been adopted in the MoM and EU-MaDE4LL projects, where the underlying assumption was to empower learners' agency. Some examples of descriptors and 'can-do' statements from the *Common Framework of Reference for Intercultural Digital Literacies* (CFRIDiL) indicates how critical, multimodal and digital literacies can be improved in intercultural scenarios, where English is one language of communication, but not necessarily the only or the most important one (see Sindoni, Adami, Karatza, Moschini et al., 2021; Sindoni, Adami, Moschini, Petroni & Karatza, 2021a).

As argued by Cope and Kalantzis, rather than creating dedicated, smart, inclusive and meaningful digital technologies, much effort has been spent so far on the *mere conversion of materiality,* for example turning 'in-person lectures (into) video lectures' (2021: 34). This Element has been designed to contest the assumption that changing materiality does not challenge mutual understanding. Quite the opposite, conversion of materiality produces a range of far-ranging medium-specific affordances that cannot be unpacked and understood by simply considering mediation as a technological matter. This is especially true when considering the ever-growing permeability of contexts, cultures, varieties and languages that the current digital mediascapes accrue. Approaches that consider processes of sense and knowledge making are compatible with multimodal and translanguaging theories of communication and, as such, should be incorporated in reformist educational agendas as they prioritize learners' agency over performance-based metrics and rubrics (Archer, 2021).

Some more steps need to be taken to explore and further expand knowledge of all the forms of sense making by increasingly large numbers of people who use video interactions daily. Further research should address the new challenges brought about by the new frontiers of mediated live communication, for example in telepresence environments, as well as in increasingly immersive learning and leisure spaces, such as the metaverse.

References

Androutsopoulos, J. (2011). From variation to heteroglossia in the study of computer-mediated discourse. In C. Thurlow & K. Mroczek, eds., *Digital Discourse: Language in the New Media*. Oxford: Oxford University Press, pp. 277–98.

Archer, A. (2021). Recognition of student resources in digital environments. In M. G. Sindoni & I. Moschini, eds., *Multimodal Literacies across Digital Learning Contexts*. London: Routledge, pp. 152–65.

Argyle, M. (1976). *Gaze and Mutual Gaze*. Cambridge: Cambridge University Press.

Argyle, M., Ingham, R., Alkema, F. & McCallin, M. (1973). The different functions of gaze. *Semiotica*, 7(1), 19–32.

Argyle, M., Furnham, A. & Graham, J. A. (1981). *Social Situations*. Cambridge: Cambridge University Press.

Autobiography of Intercultural Encounters (AIE) (2009). The Autobiography of Intercultural Encounters: Context, concepts and theories. Available at: www.coe.int/en/web/autobiography-intercultural-encounters.

Baker, C. (2011). *Foundations of Bilingual Education and Bilingualism*, 5th ed. Bristol: Multilingual Matters.

Baldry, A. (2005). *A Multimodal Approach to Text Studies in English*. Campobasso: Palladino.

Baldry, A. & Thibault, P. (2006). *Multimodal Transcription and Text Analysis: A Multimedia Toolkit and Coursebook*. London: Equinox.

Baldry A. & Thibault, P. (2020). A model for multimodal corpus construction of video genres: Phasal analysis and resource integration using OpenMWS. In N. Vasta & A. Baldry, eds., *Multiliteracy Advances and Multimodal Challenges in ELT Environments*. Udine: Forum, pp. 159–73.

Baron, N. S. (2000). *Alphabet to E-mail: How Written English Evolved and Where It's Heading*. London: Routledge.

Bateman, J. A. (2008). *Multimodality and Genre: A Foundation for the Systematic Analysis of Multimodal Documents*. London: Palgrave Macmillan.

Baynam, M. & Lee, T. K. (2019). *Translation and Translanguaging*. London: Routledge.

Benson, P. (2015). Commenting to learn: Evidence of language and intercultural learning in comments on YouTube videos. *Language Learning & Technology*, 19(3), 88–105.

Bezemer, J. & Kress, G. (2016). *Multimodality, Learning and Communication: A Social Semiotic Frame*. London: Routledge.

Birdwhistell, R. L. (1952). *Introduction to Kinesics: An Annotation System for Analysis of Body Motion and Gesture*. Washington, DC: Department of State, Foreign Service Institute.

Block, D. (2014). Moving beyond 'lingualism': Multilingual embodiment and multimodality in SLA. In S. May, ed., *The Multilingual Turn: Implications for SLA, TESOL and Bilingual Education*. London: Routledge, pp. 54–77.

Blommaert, J. (2010). *The Sociolinguistics of Globalization*. Cambridge: Cambridge University Press.

Bohannon, L. S., Herbert, A. M., Pelz, J. B. & Rantanen, E. M. (2013). Eye contact and video-mediated communication: A review. *Displays*, 34(2), 177–85.

Bojsen, H., Daryai-Hansen, P., Holmen, A. & Risager K. (eds.) (2023). *Translanguaging and Epistemological Decentring in Higher Education and Research*. Bristol: Multilingual Matters.

Busch, F. (2018). Digital writing practices and media ideologies of German adolescents. *The Mouth*, 3, 85–103.

Busch, F. & Sindoni, M. G. (2022). Metapragmatics of mode-switching: Young people's awareness of multimodal meaning making in digital interaction. In C. Groff, A. Hollington, E. Hurst-Harosh et al., eds., *Global Perspectives on Youth Language Practices*, vol. 119. Berlin: Mouton de Gruyter, pp. 245–64.

Canagarajah, S. (2013). *Translingual Practice: Global Englishes and Cosmopolitan Relations*. London: Routledge.

Canagarajah, S. (2020). Transnational work, translingual practices, and interactional sociolinguistics. *Journal of Sociolinguistics*, 24(5), 555–73.

Canagarajah, S. (2022). Challenges in decolonizing linguistics: The politics of enregisterment and the divergent uptakes of translingualism. *Educational Linguistics*, 1(1), 25–55.

Canals, L. (2021). Multimodality and translanguaging in negotiation of meaning. *Foreign Language Annals*, 54, 647–70.

Canals, L. (2022). The role of the language of interaction and translanguaging on attention to interactional feedback in virtual exchanges. *System*, 105(1), 102721.

Chen, Q. & Lin, A. (2022). Reconceptualizing semiotic resources in the eco-social system of an online language tutoring course. *Pedagogies: An International Journal*, 17(4), 348–67. https://doi.org/10.1080/1554480X.2022.2139260.

Cirillo, L. (2019). The pragmatics of air quotes in English academic presentations. *Journal of Pragmatics*, 142, 1–15.

Clabby, M. C. (2021). Comme y'all voulez: Translanguaging practices in digitally mediated communication. Unpublished MA dissertation, University of Georgia.

Code, J., Ralph, R. & Forde, K. (2020). Pandemic designs for the future: Perspectives of technology education teachers during COVID-19. *Information and Learning Sciences*, 121(5/6), 419–31. https://doi.org/10 .1108/ILS-04-2020-0112.

Coman, C., Țîru, L. G., Meseşan-Schmitz, L., Stanciu, C. & Bularca, M. C. (2020). Online teaching and learning in higher education during the coronavirus pandemic: Students' perspective. *Sustainability*, 12, 10367. https://doi .org/10.3390/su122410367.

Common European Framework of Reference for Languages: Learning, Teaching, Assessment (CEFR) (2001). The CEFR levels. Available at: www.coe.int/en/web/common-european-framework-reference-languages/ level-descriptions.

Cope, B. & Kalantzis, M. (2021). Pedagogies for digital learning: From transpositional grammar to the literacies of education. In M. G. Sindoni & I. Moschini, eds., *Multimodal Literacies across Digital Learning Contexts*. London: Routledge, pp. 34–53.

Crawford Camiciottoli, B. (2021). Analyzing attitudinal stance in OpenCourseWare lectures: An experimental mixed-method approach. In M. G. Sindoni & I. Moschini, eds., *Multimodal Literacies across Digital Learning Contexts*. London: Routledge, pp. 212–27.

Creese, A. & Blackledge, A. (2010). Translanguaging in the bilingual classroom: A pedagogy for learning and teaching? *Modern Language Journal*, 94 (1), 103–15.

Cummins, J. (2008). Teaching for transfer: Challenging the two solitudes assumption in bilingual education. In N. H. Hornberger, ed., *Encyclopedia of Language and Education*. Boston, MA: Springer, pp. 1528–38. https://doi .org/10.1007/978-0-387-30424-3_116.

de Saussure, F. [1916] (2011). *Course in General Linguistics*. Ed. by P. Meisel and H. Saussy. English translation by W. Baskin (1959). New York: Columbia University Press.

Diamantopoulou, S. & Ørevik, S. (eds.) (2022). *Multimodality in English Language Learning*. London: Routledge.

Digcomp 2.0. (2016). The Digital Competence Framework for Citizens. Available at: https://ec.europa.eu/jrc/en/digcomp.

Doherty-Sneddon, G., Anderson, A., O'Malley, C. et al. (1997). Face-to-face and video-mediated communication: A comparison of dialogue structure and task performance. *Journal of Experimental Psychology: Applied*, 3(2), 105–25. https://doi.org/10.1037/1076-898X.3.2.105.

Drąg, K. (2020). Revaluation of the proxemics code in mediatized communication. *Social Communication*, 6(1), 93–105. https://doi.org/10.2478/sc-2020-0010.

Ekman, P. & Friesen, W. E. (1969). The repertoire of nonverbal behavior: Categories, origins, usage, and coding. *Semiotica*, 1, 49–98.

Fadelli, I. (2019). Intel researchers develop an eye contact correction system for video chats. *TechExplore*, 26 June 2019. Available at: https://techxplore.com/news/2019-06-intel-eye-contact-video-chats.html.

Flewitt, R., Hampel, R., Hauck, M. & Lancaster, L. (2009). What are multimodal data and transcription? In C. Jewitt, ed., *The Handbook of Multimodal Analysis*, 1st ed. London: Routledge, pp. 40–53.

Ford, C. E. & Thompson, S. A. (1996). Interactional units in conversation: Syntactic, intonational, and pragmatic resources for the management of turns. In E. Ochs, E. A. Schegloff & S. A. Thompson, eds., *Interaction and Grammar*. Cambridge: Cambridge University Press, pp. 134–84. https://doi.org/10.1017/CBO9780511620874.003.

Friesen, N. (2014). Telepresence and tele-absence: A phenomenology of the (in)visible alien online. *Phenomenology & Practice*, 8(1), 17–31.

García, O. (2009). *Bilingual Education in the 21st Century: A Global Perspective*. Malden, MA: Wiley/Blackwell.

García, O. & Li, W. (2014). *Translanguaging: Language, Bilingualism and Education*. Basingstoke: Palgrave Macmillan.

García, O. & Lin, A. M. Y. (2016). Translanguaging in bilingual education. In O. García, A. M. Y. Lin & S. May, eds., *Bilingual and Multilingual Education. Encyclopedia of Language and Education*. Dordrecht: Springer, pp. 117–30.

Geenen, J. & Pirini, J. (2021). Interrelation: Gaze and multimodal ensembles. In I. Moschini & M. G. Sindoni, eds., *Mediation and Multimodal Meaning Making in Digital Environments*. London: Routledge, pp. 85–102.

Gershon, I. (2010a). Media ideologies. An introduction. *Journal of Linguistic Anthropology*, 20(2), 283–93.

Gershon, I. (2010b). Breaking up is hard to do: Media switching and media ideologies. *Journal of Linguistic Anthropology*, 20(2), 389–405.

Gibson, J. J. (1986) [1979]. *The Ecological Approach to Visual Perception*. Hillsdale, NJ: Lawrence Erlbaum.

Goffman, E. (1971). *Relations in Public: Microstudies of the Public Order*. London: Allen Lane, Penguin.

Goffman, E. (1981). *Forms of Talk*. Philadelphia, PA: University of Pennsylvania Press.

Goldin-Meadow, S. (1999). The development of gesture with and without speech in hearing and deaf children. In L. S. Messing & R. Campbell, eds., *Gesture, Speech and Sign*. Oxford: Oxford University Press, pp. 117–32.

Goodwin, C. (1979). The interactive construction of a sentence in natural conversation. In G. Psathas, ed., *Everyday Language: Studies in Ethnomethodology*. New York: Irvington, pp. 97–121.

Goodwin, C. (1980). Restarts, pauses, and the achievement of a state of mutual gaze at turn beginning. *Sociological Inquiry*, 50(3–4), 272–302.

Goodwin, C. (1989). *Conversational Organization: Interaction between Speakers and Hearers*. New York: Academic Press.

Goodwin, C. (2000). Action and embodiment within situated human interaction. *Journal of Pragmatics*, 32, 1489–1522.

Goodwin, C. (2013). The co-operative, transformative organization of human action and knowledge. *Journal of Pragmatics*, 46(1), 8–23.

Grand View Research (2022). *Video Conferencing Market Size, Market Share, Application Analysis, Regional Outlook, Growth Trends, Key Players, Competitive Strategies and Forecasts, 2022 to 2030*. August 2022. Available at: www.researchandmarkets.com/reports/5660013/video-conferencing-market-size-market-share#src-pos-1.

Grayson, D. & Coventry, L. (1998). The effects of visual proxemic information in video mediated communication. *ACM Special Interest Group on Computer-Human Interaction*, 30(3), 30–9.

Hall, E. T. (1966). *The Hidden Dimension*. New York: Doubleday.

Halliday, M. A. K. (1973). *Explorations in the Functions of Language*. London: Arnold.

Halliday, M. A. K. (1978). *Language as Social Semiotic*. London: Arnold.

Halliday, M. A. K. (1989). *Spoken and Written Language*. London: Oxford University Press.

Harrigan, J. A. (2005). Proxemics, kinesics and gaze. In J. A. Harrigan, R. Rosenthal & K. R. Scherer, eds., *The New Handbook of Methods in Nonverbal Behavior Research*. Oxford: Oxford University Press, pp. 137–98.

Haviland, J. B. (2004). Gesture. In A. Duranti, ed., *A Companion to Linguistic Anthropology*. Malden, MA: Blackwell, pp. 197–221.

He, M., Xiong, B. & Xia, K. (2021). Are you looking at me? Eye gazing in web video conferences. *ACM Conference Proceedings*. Available at: https://courses.ece.ubc.ca/518/previous/hit2020W/papers/group8_99750_14423175_ACM_Conference_Proceedings_Primary_Article_Template%20(2).pdf

Heath, C., Hindmarsh, J. & Luff, P. (2010). *Video in Qualitative Research: Analysing Social Interaction in Everyday Life*. London: Sage.

Heath, C. & Luff, P. (1992). Media space and communicative asymmetries: Preliminary observations of video-mediated interaction. *Journal of Human-Computer Interaction*, 7(3), 315–46.

Herring, S. C., Stein, D. & Virtanen, T. (eds.) (2013). *Handbook of Pragmatics of Computer-Mediated Communication*. Berlin: De Gruyter.

Herring, S. C. (2012). Discourse in Web 2.0: Familiar, reconfigured, and emergent. In D. Tannen & A. M. Trester, eds., *Discourse 2.0: Language and New Media*. Washington, DC: Georgetown University Press, pp. 1–25.

Hietanen, J. O., Peltola, M. J. & Hietanen, J. K. (2020). Psychophysiological responses to eye contact in a live interaction and in video call. *Psychophysiology*, 57(6), e13587. https://doi.org/10.1111/psyp.13587.

Hjulstad, J. (2016). Practices of organizing built space in videoconference-mediated interactions. *Research on Language and Social Interaction*, 49(4), 325–41.

Ho, W. Y. J. & Feng, D. W. (2022) Orchestrating multimodal resources in English language teaching: A critical study of an online English teaching video. *Pedagogies: An International Journal*, 17(4), 368–88. https://doi.org/10.1080/1554480X.2022.2139257.

Ho, W. Y. J. & Li, W. (2019). Mobilizing learning: A translanguaging view. *Chinese Semiotic Studies*, 4, 533–59. https://doi.org/10.1515/css-2019-0029.

Ho, W. Y. J. & Tai, K. W. H. (2021). Translanguaging in digital learning: The making of translanguaging spaces in online English teaching videos. *International Journal of Bilingual Education and Bilingualism*. https://doi.org/10.1080/13670050.2021.2001427.

Hutchby, I. (2001). *Conversation and Technology: From the Telephone to the Internet*. Cambridge: Polity Press.

Hutchby, I. (2014). Communicative affordances and participation frameworks in mediated interaction. *Journal of Pragmatics*, 72, 86–9.

Iedema, R. (2003). Multimodality, resemiotization: Extending the analysis of discourse as multi-semiotic practice. *Visual Communication*, 2(1), 29–57.

Jakonen, T. & Jauni, H. (2021). Mediated learning materials: Visibility checks in telepresence robot mediated classroom interaction. *Classroom Discourse*, 12(1–2), 121–45. https://doi:10.1080/19463014.2020.1808496.

Jewitt, C. (ed.) (2014). *The Handbook of Multimodal Analysis*, 2nd ed. London: Routledge.

Jewitt, C., Bezemer, J. & O'Halloran, K. L. (2016). *Introducing Multimodality*. London: Routledge.

Jones, R. H. (2020). Accounting for surveillance. *Journal of Sociolinguistics*, 24(1), 89–95.

Joshi, A., Vinay, M. & Bhaskar, P. (2021). Impact of coronavirus pandemic on the Indian education sector: Perspectives of teachers on online teaching and assessments. *Interactive Technology and Smart Education*, 18(2), 205–26. https://doi.org/10.1108/ITSE-06-2020-0087.

Kaiser, N., Henry, K. & Eyjólfsdóttir, H. (2022). Eye contact in video communication: Experiences of co-creating relationships. *Frontiers in Psychology*, 13, 852692. https://doi:10.3389/fpsyg.2022.852692.

Kendon, A. (1967). Some functions of gaze-direction in social interaction. *Acta Psychologica*, 26, 22–63.

Kendon, A. (1990a). Reflections on the study of gesture. *Visual Anthropology*, 8, 121–31.

Kendon, A. (1990b). *Conducting Interaction: Patterns of Behavior in Focused Encounters*. Cambridge: Cambridge University Press.

Kendon, A. (1997). Gesture. *Annual Review of Anthropology*, 26, 109–28.

Kendon, A. (2004). *Gesture: Visible Action as Utterance*. Cambridge: Cambridge University Press.

Kessler, M., Loewen, S. & Trego, D. (2021) Synchronous video computer-mediated communication in English language teaching. *ELT Journal*, 75(3), 371–6. https://doi.org/10.1093/elt/ccab007.

Kress, G. (2000). Design and transformation: New theories of meaning. In B. Cope & M. Kalantzis, eds., *Multiliteracies: Literacy Learning and the Design of Social Futures*. London: Routledge, pp. 155–8.

Kress, G. (2003). *Literacy in the New Media Age*. London: Routledge.

Kress, G. (2005). Gains and losses: New forms of texts, knowledge, and learning, *Computers and Composition*, 22(1), 5–22.

Kress, G. (2009). What is a mode? In C. Jewitt, ed., *The Routledge Handbook of Multimodal Analysis*, 1st ed. London: Routledge, pp. 54–67.

Kress, G. (2010). *Multimodality: A Social Semiotic Approach to Contemporary Communication*. London: Routledge.

Kress, G. & van Leeuwen, T. (2001). *Multimodal Discourse: The Modes and Media of Contemporary Communication*. London: Arnold.

Kress, G. & van Leeuwen, T. (2020). *Reading Images: A Grammar of Visual Design*, 3rd ed. [1996, 1st ed.]. London: Routledge.

Kress, G., Jewitt, C., Ogborn, J. & Tsatsarelis, C. (2001). *Multimodal Teaching and Learning: The Rhetorics of the Science Classroom*. London: Continuum.

Laver, J. (1975). Communicative functions of phatic communion. In A. Kendon, R. Harris & M. R. Key, eds., *The Organisation of Behaviour in Face-to-Face Interaction*. The Hague: Mouton, pp. 215–38.

Legewie, N. & Nassauer, A. (2022). *Video Data Analysis: How to Use 21st Century Video in the Social Sciences.* London: Sage.

Li, C. (2002). The role of gaze in meaning negotiation episodes in video synchronous computer-mediated interactions. *Journal of China Computer-Assisted Language Learning*, 2(1), 100–25. https://doi.org/10.1515/jccall-2022-0005.

Li, D. (2022). The shift to online classes during the Covid-19 pandemic: Benefits, challenges, and required improvements from the students' perspective. *Electronic Journal of e-Learning*, 20(1), 1–18.

Li, W. (2011). Moment analysis and translanguaging space: Discursive construction of identities by multilingual Chinese youth in Britain. *Journal of Pragmatics*, 43(5), 1222–235.

Li, W. (2018). Translanguaging as a practical theory of language. *Applied Linguistics*, 39(1), 9–30. https://doi.org/10.1093/applin/amx039.

Li, W. & Zhu, H. (2013). Translanguaging identities and ideologies: Creating transnational space through flexible multilingual practices amongst Chinese university students in the UK. *Applied Linguistics*, 34(5), 516–35.

Li, W. & Zhu, H. (2019). Tranßcripting: Playful subversion with Chinese characters. *International Journal of Multilingualism*, 16(2), 145–61.

Licoppe, C. (2009). Recognizing mutual 'proximity' at a distance: Weaving together mobility, sociality and technology. *Journal of Pragmatics*, 41(10), 1924–37.

Licoppe, C. & Morel, J. (2014). Mundane video directors in interaction: Showing one's environment in Skype and mobile video calls. In M. Broth, E. Laurier & L. Mondada, eds., *Studies of Video Practices: Video at Work.* London: Routledge, pp. 135–60.

Lim, F. V. (2021). *Designing Learning with Embodied Teaching: Perspectives from Multimodality.* London: Routledge.

Lin, A. (2015). Egalitarian bi/multilingualism and trans-semiotizing in a global world. In E. Wayne, B. Sovicheth & O. García, eds., *The Handbook of Bilingual and Multilingual Education*. Malden, MA: Wiley/Blackwell, pp. 19–37.

Lin, A. (2018). Theories of trans/languaging and trans-semiotizing: Implications for content-based education classrooms. *International Journal of Bilingual Education and Bilingualism*, 22(1), 5–16.

Maher, D. (2022). The use of video conferencing to support pre-service teachers during Covid-19. *A Retrospective of Teaching, Technology, and Teacher Education during the COVID-19 Pandemic*, 19, 19–24.

Malabarba, T., Oliveira Mendes, A. C. & de Souza, J. (2022). Multimodal resolution of overlapping talk in video-mediated L2 instruction. *Languages*, 7, 154. https://doi.org/10.3390/languages7020154.

Martinec, R. (2004). Gestures that co-occur with speech as a systematic resource: The realization of experiential meaning in indexes. *Social Semiotics*, 14(2), 193–213.

Mateus, J. C., Andrada, P., González-Cabrera, C. & Ugalde, C. (2022). Teachers' perspectives for a critical agenda in media education post COVID-19: A comparative study in Latin America. *Comunicar*, 30(70), 9–19.

McIntyre, N. A., Mainhard, M. & Klassen, R. M. (2017). 'Are you looking to teach?' Cultural, temporal and dynamic insights into expert teacher gaze. *Learning and Instruction*, 49, 41–53.

McNeill, D. (1992). *Hand and Mind: What Gestures Reveal about Thought*. Chicago: Chicago University Press.

McNeill, D. (2005). *Gesture and Thought*. Chicago: Chicago University Press.

Mondada, L. (2016). Challenges of multimodality: Language and the body in social interaction. *Journal of Sociolinguistics*, 20(3), 336–66.

Mondada, L. & Oloff, F. (2011). Gestures in overlap: The situated establishment of speakership. In G. Stam & M. Ishino, eds., *Integrating Gestures: The Interdisciplinary Nature of Gesture*. Amsterdam: John Benjamins, pp. 321–38.

Monk, A. F. & Gale, C. (2002). A look is worth a thousand words: Full gaze awareness in video-mediated conversation. *Discourse Processes*, 33(3), 257–78.

Mora, R. A., Tian, Z. & Harman, R. (2022a). *Translanguaging and Multimodality. Special Issue of Pedagogies: An International Journal*, 4.

Mora, R. A., Tian, Z. & Harman, R. (2022b). Translanguaging and multimodality as flow, agency, and a new sense of advocacy in and from the Global South. *Special Issue of Pedagogies: An International Journal*, 4, 271–81.

New London Group (1996). A pedagogy of multiliteracies: Designing social futures. *Harvard Educational Review*, 66(1), 60–93.

Norris, S. (2004). *Analyzing Multimodal Interaction: A Methodological Framework*. London: Routledge.

O'Conaill, B., Whittaker, S. & Wilbur, S. (1993). Conversations over video conferences: An evaluation of the spoken aspects of video-mediated communication. *Human–Computer Interaction*, 8(4), 389–428. https://doi.org/10.1207/s15327051hci0804_4.

O'Halloran, K. L. (ed.) (2004). *Multimodal Discourse Analysis: Systemic Functional Perspectives*. London: Continuum.

O'Halloran, K. L. (2008). Systemic functional-multimodal discourse analysis (SF-MDA): Constructing ideational meaning using language and visual imagery. *Visual Communication*, 7(4), 443–75. https://doi.org/10.1177/1470357208096210.

O'Halloran, K. L. (2006). *Mathematical Discourse: Language, Symbolism and Visual Images*. London: Bloomsbury.

O'Toole, M. (1994). *The Language of Displayed Art*, 1st ed. London: Routledge.

Ou, A. W., Gu, M. M. & Lee, J. C-K. (2022). Learning and communication in online international higher education in Hong Kong: ICT-mediated translanguaging competence and virtually translocal identity. *Journal of Multilingual and Multicultural Development*. https://doi.org/10.1080/01434632.2021.2021210.

Paech, V. (2012). The inevitable exile: A missing link in online community discourse. In T. Brabazon, ed., *Digital Dialogues and Community 2.0*. Oxford: Chandos Publishing, pp. 11–42.

Panopto (2022). Synchronous vs. asynchronous communication: What's the difference? *Panopto*, 15 July 2022. Available at: www.panopto.com/blog/learning-and-development-asynchronous-vs-synchronous-video-communications-whats-the-difference/.

Paulus, T., Warren, A. & Lester, J. N. (2016). Applying conversation analysis methods to online talk: A literature review. *Discourse, Context and Media*, 12, 1–10. https://doi.org/10.1016/j.dcm.2016.04.001.

Peng, J.-I. (2019). The roles of multimodal pedagogic effects and classroom environment in willingness to communicate in English. *System*, 82, 161–73.

Pennycook, A. & Otsuji, E. (2015). *Metrolingualism: Language in the City*. London: Routledge.

Pink, S. (2007). *Doing Visual Ethnography*. London: Sage.

Rapanta, C., Botturi, L., Goodyear, P., Guardia, L. & Koole, M. (2020). Online university teaching during and after the Covid-19 crisis: Refocusing teacher presence and learning activity. *Postdigital Science and Education*, 2, 923–45. https://link.springer.com/article/10.1007/s42438-020-00155-y#article-info.

Ravelli, L. & McMurtrie, R. J. (2015). *Multimodality in the Built Environment: Spatial Discourse Analysis*. London: Routledge.

Recktenwald, D. (2017). Toward a transcription and analysis of live streaming on Twitch. *Journal of Pragmatics*, 115, 68–81.

Rintel, S. (2015). *Conversation Analysis of Video-Mediated Communication: Interactional Repair of Distortion in Long-Distance Couples' Video Calls*. London: Sage.

Rosenbaun, L., Rafaeli, S. & Kurzon, D. (2016a). Participation frameworks in multiparty video chats cross-modal exchanges in public Google Hangouts. *Journal of Pragmatics*, 94, 29–46.

Rosenbaun, L., Rafaeli, S. & Kurzon, D. (2016b). Blurring the boundaries between domestic and digital spheres: Competing engagements in public Google Hangouts. *Pragmatics*, 26(2), 291–314.

Rossano, F. (2012). Gaze behavior in face-to-face interaction. PhD thesis, Radboud University Nijmegen, The Netherlands.

Rossano, F. (2013). Gaze in conversation. In J. Sidnell & T. Stivers, eds., *The Handbook of Conversation Analysis*. Malden, MA: Wiley/Blackwell, pp. 308–29.

Sacks, H., Schegloff, E. A. & Jefferson, G. (1974). A simplest systematics for the organization of turn-taking for conversation. *Language*, 50(4), 696–735.

Satar, H. M. (2013). Multimodal language learner interactions via desktop videoconferencing within a framework of social presence: Gaze. *ReCALL*, 25(1), 122–42. https://doi.org/10.1017/S0958344012000286.

Scheflen, A. E. (1964). The significance of posture in communication systems. *Psychiatry*, 27(4), 316–31. https://doi.org/10.1080/00332747.1964.11023403.

Schegloff, E. A. (1984). On some gestures' relation to talk. In J. Maxwell Atkinson & J. Heritage, eds., *Structures of Social Action: Studies in Conversation Analysis*, Cambridge: Cambridge University Press, pp. 266–95.

Schiffrin, D. (1986). *Discourse Markers. Studies in Interactional Sociolinguistics*, 5, Cambridge: Cambridge University Press.

Schreiber, B. R. (2015). 'I am what I am': Multilingual identity and digital translanguaging. *Language Learning & Technology*, 19(3), 69–87.

Scollon, R. (2001). *Mediated Discourse: The Nexus of Practice*. London: Routledge.

Shih, Y-C. (2014). Communication strategies in a multimodal virtual communication context. *System*, 42, 34–47.

Sindoni, M. G. (2011). Online conversations: A sociolinguistic investigation into young adults' use of videochats. *Classroom Discourse*, 2, 219–35.

Sindoni, M. G. (2012). Mode-switching: How oral and written modes alternate in videochats. In M. Cambria, C. Arizzi & F. Coccetta, eds., *Web Genres and Web Tools: With Contributions from the Living Knowledge Project*. Como-Pavia: Ibis, pp. 141–53.

Sindoni, M. G. (2013). *Spoken and Written Discourse in Online Interactions: A Multimodal Approach*. London: Routledge.

Sindoni, M. G. (2014). Through the looking glass: A social semiotic and linguistic perspective on the study of video chats. *Text & Talk*, 34, 325–47.

Sindoni, M. G. (2018). 'Of course I'm married!' Communicative strategies and transcription-related issues in video-mediated interactions. In P. Garcés-Conejos Blitvich & P. Bou, eds., *Analyzing Digital*

Discourse: New Insights and Future Directions. Basingstoke: Palgrave Macmillan, pp. 71–103.

Sindoni, M. G. (2019). Mode-switching in video-mediated interaction: Integrating linguistic phenomena into multimodal transcription tasks. *Linguistics and Education*, 62, 100738.

Sindoni, M. G. & Moschini, I. (2021a). Discourses on discourse, shifting contexts and digital media. In M. G. Sindoni & I. Moschini, eds, 'What's past is prologue': Continuity and change in theories and methodologies on discourse in multimodal digital texts and practices. Special issue of *Discourse, Context & Media*, 43, 100534.

Sindoni, M. G. & Moschini, I. (2021b). Towards a framework for video mediated 'Cooper-action': Discourse practices, bonding and distance in synchronous and asynchronous digital video spaces. In I. Moschini & M. G. Sindoni, eds., *Mediation and Multimodal Meaning Making in Digital Environments.* London: Routledge, pp. 205–28.

Sindoni, M. G., Adami, E., Karatza, S., Marenzi, I., Petroni, S. & Rocca, M. (2019). *Common Framework of Reference for Intercultural Digital Literacies.* Available at: www.eumade4ll.eu/wp-content/uploads/2020/02/cfridil-framework-linked-fin1.pdf.

Sindoni, M. G., Adami, E., Karatza, S. & Moschini, I. (2021). An introduction to the *Common Framework of Reference for Intercultural Digital Literacies*: Learning as meaning-making and assessment as recognition. In S. Ørevik & S. Diamantopoulou, eds., *Multimodality in English Language Learning.* London: Routledge, pp. 221–37.

Sindoni, M. G., Adami, E., Moschini, I., Petroni, S. & Karatza, S. (2021). The theory and practice of the *Common Framework of Reference for Intercultural Digital Literacies* (CFRIDiL). In M. G. Sindoni & I. Moschini, eds,. *Multimodal Literacies across Digital Learning Contexts.* London: Routledge, pp. 166–84.

Statista (2022). Work from home & remote work. Available at: www .statista.com/study/66179/dossier-work-from-home-and-remote-work/.

Streeck, J., Goodwin, C. & LeBaron, C. D. (2011). *Embodied Interaction: Language and Body in the Material World.* Cambridge: Cambridge University Press.

Swan, P. K., Richardson, J. C., Ice, P., Garrison, D. R., Cleveland-Innes, M. & Arbaugh, J. B. (2008). Validating a measurement tool of presence in online communities of inquiry. *E-Mentor*, 2(24), 1–12.

Sweeney, E. & Zhu, H. (2010). Accommodating toward your audience: Do native speakers of English know how to accommodate their communication strategies toward nonnative speakers of English? *The Journal of Business Communication*, 47(4), 477–504.

Tai, K. W. H. & Li, W. (2021). Constructing playful talk through translanguaging in English Medium Instruction mathematics classrooms. *Applied Linguistics*, 42(4), 607–40. https://doi.org/10.1093/applin/amaa043.

Tan, S., Wiebrands, M., O'Halloran, K. L. & Wignell, P. (2020). Analysing student engagement with 360-degree videos through multimodal data analytics and user annotations. *Technology, Pedagogy and Education*, 29(5), 593–612.

Thibault, P. J. (2017). The reflexivity of human languaging and Nigel Love's two orders of language. *Language Sciences*, 61, 74–85.

Tschaepe, M. (2020). Seeing and viewing through a postdigital pandemic: Shifting from physical proximity to scopic mediation. *Postdigit Science Education*, 2, 757–71.

van Leeuwen, T. (1999). *Speech, Music and Sound*. London: Palgrave.

van Leeuwen, T. & Jewitt, C. (eds.) (2001). *The Handbook of Visual Analysis*. London: Sage.

Vasta, N. & Baldry, A. (eds.) (2020). *Multiliteracy Advances and Multimodal Challenges in ELT Environments*. Udine: Forum.

Vertegaal, R. & Ding, Y. (2002). Explaining effects of eye gaze on mediated group conversations: Amount or synchronization? In E. F. Churchill, J. McCarthy, C. Neuwirth & T. Rodden, eds., *Proceedings of the 2002 ACM Conference on Computer Supported Cooperative Work*. New York: ACM Press, pp. 41–8.

Wang, X., Liu, T., Wang, J. & Tian, J. (2022). Understanding learner continuance intention: A comparison of live video learning, pre-recorded video learning and hybrid video learning in Covid-19 pandemic. *International Journal of Human–Computer Interaction*, 38(3), 263–81.

Williams, C. (1994). Arfarniad o Ddulliau Dysgu ac Addysgu yng Nghyddestun Addysg Uwchradd Ddwyieithog. [An evaluation of teaching and learning methods in the context of bilingual secondary education]. PhD thesis, University of Wales, Bangor.

Zhang, L. J. (2022). Deepening the understanding of translanguaging as a practical theory of language: A conversation with Professor Li Wei. *RELC Journal*, 1–8. https://doi.org/10.1177/00336882221139894.

Zhu, H. (2013) *Exploring Intercultural Communication: Language in Action*. London: Routledge.

Zhu, H. (2015). Negotiation as the way of engagement in intercultural and lingua franca communication: Frames of reference and interculturality. *Journal of English as a Lingua Franca*, 4(1), 63–90.

Zhu, H. (2019) *Exploring Intercultural Communication: Language in Action*, 2nd ed. London: Routledge.

Zhu, H. & Kramsch, C. (eds.) (2016). Symbolic power and conversational inequality in intercultural communication. *Applied Linguistics Review*, 7 (4), 375–83.

Zhu H., Li, W. & Jankowicz-Pytel, D. (2020). Translanguaging and embodied teaching and learning: Lessons from a multilingual karate club in London, *International Journal of Bilingual Education and Bilingualism*, 23(1), 65–80.

Acknowledgements

My research on video-mediated interactions over the past fifteen years would not exist without the countless contributions by participants and learners who have discussed, commented, reflected and shared their video data with me. I have conducted digital field observations, pre- and post interviews with people coming from the five continents and I have counted approximately forty-seven different nationalities involved in this decade-long project so far. When I mention the number of 'nationalities', I am actually crudely banalizing the rich and multifaceted multicultural and translingual background of people from all paths of life who big-heartedly shared their experiences, observations and insights with me. I truly believe that reflecting on spontaneous interactions, be they mediated or otherwise, significantly improves the quality of our relationships and the value we give to our time.

My profound gratitude goes to Anthony Baldry, a good friend and a great scholar, who first sparked my interest in multimodal studies and has involved me in an ongoing discussion on the semiosis of communication. Words cannot express how much I owe to his intellectual rigour and generous advice over many years.

I wish to thank Zhu Hua and Li Wei for their constructive feedback and patience throughout the process. I also would like to thank Isabel Collins and Adam Hooper at Cambridge University Press for their support and Vibhu Prathima Palanisame at Integra Software Services for her hard work on the manuscript.

Listing the names of other colleagues and friends who have variously contributed to my research on VMI would lead me too far, but I am symbolically thanking each of them.

One final personal note: heartfelt thanks go to my family and close friends for being there for me, always.

Cambridge Elements ⁼

Applied Linguistics

Li Wei

University College London

Li Wei is Chair of Applied Linguistics at the UCL Institute of Education, University College London (UCL), and Fellow of Academy of Social Sciences, UK. His research covers different aspects of bilingualism and multilingualism. He was the founding editor of the following journals: *International Journal of Bilingualism* (Sage), *Applied Linguistics Review* (De Gruyter), *Language, Culture and Society* (Benjamins), *Chinese Language and Discourse* (Benjamins) and *Global Chinese* (De Gruyter), and is currently Editor of the *International Journal of Bilingual Education and Bilingualism* (Taylor and Francis). His books include the *Blackwell Guide to Research Methods in Bilingualism and Multilingualism* (with Melissa Moyer) and *Translanguaging: Language, Bilingualism and Education* (with Ofelia Garcia) which won the British Association of Applied Linguistics Book Prize.

Zhu Hua

University College London

Zhu Hua is Professor of Language Learning and Intercultural Communication at the UCL Institute of Education, University College London (UCL) and is a Fellow of Academy of Social Sciences, UK. Her research is centred around multilingual and intercultural communication. She has also studied child language development and language learning. She is book series co-editor for *Routledge Studies in Language and Intercultural Communication* and *Cambridge Key Topics in Applied Linguistics*, and Forum and Book Reviews Editor of *Applied Linguistics* (Oxford University Press).

About the Series

Mirroring the *Cambridge Key Topics in Applied Linguistics*, this Elements series focuses on the key topics, concepts and methods in Applied Linguistics today. It revisits core conceptual and methodological issues in different subareas of Applied Linguistics. It also explores new emerging themes and topics. All topics are examined in connection with real-world issues and the broader political, economic and ideological contexts.

Cambridge Elements ≡

Applied Linguistics

Printed in the United States
by Baker & Taylor Publisher Services